PRINCIPLED
MINISTRY

PRINCIPLED MINISTRY

A Guidebook for
CATHOLIC CHURCH LEADERS

LOUGHLAN SOFIELD, S.T.
—— and ——
CARROLL JULIANO, S.H.C.J.

ave maria press AmP notre dame, indiana

Founded in 1865, Ave Maria Press is a ministry of the Indiana Province of Holy Cross.

www.avemariapress.com

ISBN-10 1-59471-263-8   ISBN-13 978-1-59471-263-0

Cover image © Stockbyte.

Cover and text design by John R. Carson.

Printed and bound in the United States of America.

Library of Congress Cataloging-in-Publication Data

Sofield, Loughlan.
  Principled ministry : a guidebook for Catholic church
leaders / Loughlan Sofield, and Carroll Juliano.
      p. cm.
  Includes bibliographical references and index.
  ISBN-13: 978-1-59471-263-0 (pbk. : alk. paper)
  ISBN-10: 1-59471-263-8 (pbk. : alk. paper)
  1. Christian leadership--Catholic Church. I. Juliano, Carroll. II. Title.
BX1803.S64 2011
253.088'282--dc22
                    2010049280

This book is dedicated to my mentors and friends
who taught me everything I know about leadership.
James Gill, S.J., MD
Angelo D'Agostino, S.J., MD

And to my friends:
Anne Basener
Mimi MacNamee
Mary Anne Simpson
Charlene Schulcz
Claire Smith

◊ ◊ ◊

*'There is nothing on this earth more to be prized than true
friendship.'*
—Saint Thomas Aquinas

Contents

Foreword

I am honored to write this foreword to such a timely and important aid for ministers in the Catholic Church. The reader of this book has the opportunity to acquire wisdom that will bring enlightenment to his or her personal experience of Church ministry and gain insights for a greater effectiveness in training others as Church leaders.

Sr. Carroll Juliano, S.H.C.J., and Brother Loughlan Sofield, S.T., have traveled the world and have shared with so many others basic principles of ministry that are needed for Church leaders. In the pages ahead, they give insights that are simple, profound, practical, and based on solid spirituality, the teachings of the Church, and good pastoral counseling. You will have the opportunity to reflect on their writings as you examine your own ministry and strengthen your leadership skills.

All of us, no matter how long we have been involved in active ministry, are eager to sharpen our skills, to grow closer to Christ who is shepherd and teacher and to reflect his leadership in all that we do. Sr. Carroll and Br. Loughlan's reflections will be a valuable resource in helping one accomplish this reality, specifically in expanding your own leadership capabilities and challenging others to use their gifts in a like fashion.

There are many books available that focus on the skills and qualities of leaders. This book offers a new lens through which to look at leadership for ministry—thirty concise principles. As we study these principles and live them, we will become more like Christ the Good Shepherd, and reflect his mind and heart in our daily lives as co-workers in the vineyard of the Lord.

Thank you for your ministry. Thank you for reading about, applying, and living these principles that give much needed direction to what God calls us to do in our roles as ministers of his Church.

Gregory Michael Aymond
Archbishop of New Orleans

Preface

*If your actions inspire others to dream more, to learn more, to
do more and to be more than they are, then you are a leader.*
—John Quincy Adams

Church leadership, like all leadership, is multidimensional—
an amalgam of many different components. In many ways,
effective leadership is similar to being a good chef, knowing the
right amounts of spices and other ingredients necessary to create a *pièce de resistance*. Effective leadership in the Church requires
ingredients like a balanced mixture of sound theory and a carefully honed skill set; a mature spirituality and the accompanying
capacity for theological reflection; healthy relationships; unique
qualities; and at least a dash of charisma. In our earlier book,
The Collaborative Leader, we addressed many of the key ingredients
necessary to be an effective leader in the Church today by focusing on the unique *qualities and tasks* of Christian leaders in a variety of settings. We have found that the charismatic dimension of
effective leadership is often a more difficult component of good
leadership to grasp.

In general, charisma is the power of a leader to attract others to follow. Jesus was a charismatic leader who attracted his
disciples to follow him in pursuit of the Kingdom of God, even
as their natural instincts and acquisitive natures were wary of

the direction in which he drew them. Effective Church leaders—principled ministers—each have a specific, positive dream, vision, or goal. This is something that energizes and motivates them. They are so energized by these dreams that they motivate others to follow them in actualizing it. For Church leaders, that driving goal is always focused on the life and ministry of the Church, and its intended purpose is to further the mission of Jesus Christ.

There are, of course, charismatic leaders who exert evil power over those that follow them. One obvious example is Adolf Hitler, by all accounts a very charismatic leader who led many of his fellow Germans in pursuit of the vision and goals of the Nazi Party. Another example is the religious cult leader Jimmy Jones, founder and director of the Peoples Temple, who led 900 of his followers to mass suicide on November 18, 1978, in Jonestown, Guyana. Irvin Yalom, a therapist and group researcher, has indicated that charismatic leaders with evil intent, especially those inclined toward narcissism, are effective in as much as they attract followers. But of course, their leadership is used to destroy, rather than to bring life.

Catholic Church leaders, as we are describing them in this book, are those ministers, ordained and lay, who are in positions of helping individuals or groups within the Church move toward some ecclesial goal or set of goals. These goals, in pursuit of a particular vision and a clearly defined mission, can be personal, apostolic, or communal. Consequently, the range of Catholic Church leaders runs the gamut from volunteer leaders of parish activities, to pastoral counselors, ministers, and associates, to the administrative heads of organizations, schools, parishes, or dioceses. We have identified thirty leadership principles that we believe have practical applications for anyone doing ministry within that broad range of leadership. We have gleaned these principles from our experiences in direct pastoral ministries and in assisting with the professional development of other Church leaders.

In each chapter we identify and describe several principles, offer negative and positive examples of the principles at work, and invite you to stop and think through three or more related reflection questions. The principles are in no particular order, but simply organized under four broad themes. You can read this book cover to cover or use it as a reference resource by choosing a particular principle that is needed at a given time for a specific situation. The ancillary tool, *Principle Ministry Workbook*, available for free download at www.avemariapress.com, will further assist you with integrating these principles into your particular ministry and leadership style. It contains all the reflection questions posed for each principle with space to write down your responses.

Two umbrella principles encompass all the others contained in this book. These flow from what we said about charismatic leaders, and in them we distill the foundations of this book: *Leaders must be people of vision* and *leaders must have a passionate and energizing commitment to that vision*. The principles we present may at times seem almost simplistic. However, it is often the simple that we most easily overlook. When my mother, a high school graduate, reached the age of sixty-five, she attended a local college that offered free tuition to senior citizens. She decided to take Psychology 101. After one semester, when asked if she was returning for the second semester, she simply replied, 'No, it's all common sense.' Most effective leadership principles are, to a significant degree, common sense. However, common sense does not mean simplistic solutions.

Effective leaders, in Church as well as in other spheres, eschew applying simple solutions to complex issues. We have encountered leaders who propose, with great certitude, one-dimensional answers to extremely intricate situations. For example, we have heard Church leaders ascribe all problems to the issue of power struggles. Would that life and leadership were that simple!

Rarely will you reach favorable results by applying a single principle to what are invariably complex ecclesial matters. Leadership, as we mentioned in the opening paragraph, is multidimensional. Becoming a principled and effective minister in the Catholic Church today requires the skill and discernment needed to select a number of leadership principles to utilize in any given situation. Only then will you be equipped to lead the People of God in their work of building up the Kingdom.

Recently, we encountered a man who held a deep conviction in a single principle: The role of the leader is to create a climate that is conducive to dialogue. His approach to leadership was to be a sympathetic person, who by his non-threatening, but direct manner created a climate of comfort, safety, and security in which others could flourish. He described a work situation that was causing him great frustration. In spite of his best efforts to create a safe climate, he was unable to encourage one of his managerial employees to engage in dialogue. This manager was creating problems in the work situation that were having a negative impact on other workers and on the productivity of the staff. When the manager was confronted, he would generally retreat into self-defensive monologues, justifying his every action. He did not seem able to either hear or comprehend why others found his behavior objectionable. After discussion with the leader, we encouraged him to utilize another principle: Assess the desire and capacity to change. Failure to consider this would only lead to greater frustration, because expecting change in the other when there is neither the desire nor the capacity to change only leads to frustration.

The Old Testament counsels that the people will perish when there is no vision (Proverbs 29:18). Effective leaders are vision makers, who make things happen because of their commitment to their vision and ability to attract others to join them.

The following story from India dramatically portrays the need for leaders to possess a strong sense of commitment, risk, and sacrifice:

> After much prayer, Guru Nanak, the founder of Sikhism, asked that ten members be appointed as gurus who would act as leaders of various dimensions of the religion. One of the gurus was Gobind Singh. As Singh aged, he realized that it was important to identify his successor. He called all the Sikhs together and announced that he would need three leaders who were willing to make a commitment to the organizational structure of the faith. The first person to volunteer was led away to a tent. The swish of a blade was heard and one of Gobind's assistants exited the tent holding a bowl of blood and poured it on the earth. The request for two more volunteers was made. The second volunteer came forward and the scene was repeated, the swish of a blade followed by the pouring of the blood on the earth. Not surprisingly, it took much longer to locate a third volunteer. But eventually the scenario was repeated, after which, to the surprise of the assembled mass, the three volunteers emerged from the tent. Three animals had been slain and Gobind had located three leaders who were willing to make the ultimate sacrifice for the sake of the faith and those who professed it.

It is, of course, rare for Catholic leaders to be summoned to make the ultimate sacrifice of one's own life for the sake of the faith. Yet much is asked of you. *Principled Ministry* is designed to help you in becoming the Christian leader you feel called to be as you tackle the work set before you. We suggest you keep a log, choosing one principle a day and using it to assess how you do as a leader that day in your particular ministry. Use the downloadable workbook to help track your progress. This will help turn leadership theory into practical skills for effective ministry.

This book is dotted with real-life examples that are used to illustrate the thirty principles we present as well as some of our commentary. Some of these examples are drawn from the personal experiences of the one or the other co-author and we have chosen to use the preposition 'I' in these cases without identifying which of the authors is involved. We chose this method to avoid the intrusiveness of identifying from which of us the stories come.

We pray that this book will assist you in becoming the leader God has called you to be and the principled minister that the Church so urgently needs.

◊ ◊ ◊

To access the Principled Ministry Workbook, *go to avemariapress.com and search for the book title,* Principled Ministry. *Once on the book product page, click the download button. You are welcome to print the 00-page workbook, free of additional charge.*

The Ministry of Jesus: Pre-eminent Model for Church Leadership

◇◇

Jesus is the pre-eminent model for all Christian leaders. His leadership emanated from his relationship with the Father, was marked by certain well-defined characteristics, and was oriented toward mission.

Jesus' Relationship with the Father

Jesus' leadership emerged from his relationship with the Father. Throughout his life, Jesus not only modeled and witnessed the need to be in constant oneness with his heavenly Father, but also challenged his disciples and followers to this same depth of communion. Christian leaders must be, first and foremost, men and women of prayer, through which we come to realize our own intimate union with God. Our prayer must fit our lives as busy, often crisis-oriented, leaders and so needs to be distinctively styled to our individual personalities, spiritual temperaments, and ministry settings.

During a retreat for leaders of national Church organizations, certain characteristics for a spirituality of leadership emerged:

- Leadership is rooted in a deep, personal relationship with God.
- Spirituality is incarnational, embracing the whole of a ministry leader's life.
- A spirituality of leadership has to embrace the lives of administrators. This is strikingly different from the spirituality that nurtured these ministers when they were more directly involved in pastoral (versus administrative) ministry.
- One overriding question, 'Where and how is God calling me?' guides a leader's life.

These leaders were a source of inspiration and edification for us. They witnessed in very concrete and explicit ways what it means to be prayerful and to root one's ministry and identity as a leader in one's relationship to our triune God.

Characteristics of the Ministry of Jesus

Those who espouse to lead as Jesus did should reflect on the characteristics that he evidenced as a leader. First, he was compassionate or merciful and challenged his followers to be the same. Compassion seems to epitomize all that Jesus was and did. Perhaps the ministry of Jesus is best summed up in this passage from Matthew's Gospel:

> Then Jesus went about all the cities and villages, teaching in their synagogues, and proclaiming the good news of the kingdom, and curing every disease and every sickness. When he saw the crowds, he had compassion for them, because they were harassed and helpless, like sheep without a shepherd. Then he said to his disciples, 'The harvest is plentiful, but the laborers are few; therefore ask the Lord of the harvest to send out laborers into his harvest.'
>
> **—Matthew 9:35–38**

In his encyclical *Redemptoris Missio* (Mission of the Redeemer), Pope John Paul II reminds us of two primary activities of Jesus in the scriptures: healing and forgiving. Like compassion or mercy, these point to the essence of who Jesus was and to the heart of his ministry. Jesus is presented to us as a man who seems almost obsessed with the desire to heal. He sought out not only those who were physically ill, but also the poor, lonely, spiritually broken, or socially outcast and made it a priority to heal them.

Be merciful, just as your Father is merciful
—Luke 6:36

The scriptures are also replete with concrete examples of Jesus as a person of forgiveness. Even in the very last moments before his death, while his body was racked with the pain inflicted on him by his tormentors, he asked his heavenly Father to forgive those who had crucified him.

While Jesus healed and forgave, he also empowered people around him. So much of his early ministry was gathering and teaching his followers to do as he did. Truly charismatic, his model of leadership was one of calling, forming, and sending.

Jesus' Orientation toward Mission

Jesus was mission oriented. He always had the final end in view and worked consistently to gather a group of disciples, share with them his vision of the Kingdom, and establish them in their role fostering that Kingdom. He led his followers through the cycle of prayer to action toward the Kingdom.

Christian leaders are called to be prayerful people. They are to study the life of their leader, Jesus, and try to emulate his values and behavior. Ultimately, Christian leaders are focused on mission and extending the Kingdom of God.

To be a Christian leader means to mirror Jesus: to grow in a deep, personal love of God; to be compassionate, especially to those less fortunate; to be a disciple of healing and forgiveness; and to be mission oriented.

Stop and Think

What characterizes my relationship with God?

In what concrete ways does that relationship form and direct my leadership?

Does my spirituality fit my life style?

Is my ministry characterized by compassion, healing, and forgiveness?

What is the specific mission to which I am committed?

The Self-Defined Leader

◇◇◇

When we conduct workshops for Catholic educational leaders, we invite them to imagine meeting their current students twenty years after graduation. We ask them to describe how they would like to see these students develop as adults by answering three questions: What would your students be doing with their lives? What would be their values? What would make you most proud of them?

The response is generally consistent. These educators want to see their students making a difference in the world; being caring, compassionate people; and being people of integrity—women and men who live their deeply held Christian values.

After listening to their responses, we offer these educators the simplest approach to having their hopes become reality, which is *work on self-definition*. According to Edwin Freidman, the systems analyst, the best approach for leaders who desire to change and motivate others is to work on self-definition. Self-definition implies that the surest way to change others is to focus on what needs to be changed in oneself.

There are three things any leader can potentially change—oneself, the other, and the situation. Generally, leaders don't have the power or authority to change most problematic situations. Focusing on changing another almost inevitably leads to frustration. That leaves only one avenue, changing oneself, including one's attitudes, beliefs, and approaches to people and situations. Ironically, changing oneself often results in a change in the other. The first step toward self-definition is a desire and conscious choice to spend significant time in personal reflection, defining who you are and who you want to become. Second, it requires a completely honesty assessment of oneself. And finally, self-definition requires feedback from those you trust about who you are as a leader in ministry.

In addition to Freidman, others have argued for an emphasis on self-definition. Pope Paul VI put it very simply and directly in his apostle exhortation *Evangelii Nuntiandi* (On Evangelization in the Modern World) when he taught that people listen more willingly to witnesses than to teachers. When they do listen to teachers, it is because they are witnesses. The educational leaders mentioned earlier will see their graduates achieve what they hope to the extent that faculty and staff *model* the qualities and characteristics that they desire in their students.

The psychologist Abraham Maslow stressed that effective leaders are characterized by two distinct attributes: they model and they challenge. Scientific icon Marie Curie also spoke of the need for self-definition in describing her lived philosophy: 'You cannot hope to build a better world without improving the individuals. To that end each of us must work for his or her own improvement, and at the same time share a general responsibility for all humanity.'

In our experience working with Church leaders, we have noted that five attributes consistently emerge as areas requiring self-definition and self-growth:

1. Developing high self-esteem
2. Living one's Christian values
3. Fostering an attitude of zeal and hope
4. Being compassionate
5. Maintaining integrity

Self-esteem seems to be the platform upon which the other attributes build. In general, the higher the level of self-esteem, the more effective a person will be as a leader. But self-esteem is a fragile quality that is never fully achieved but always in process. Church leaders, like all leaders, bear the responsibility for building and maintaining their own self-esteem. In much of our culture, five general criteria are used for judging one's self esteem.

- Competence (what one accomplishes)
- Significance (what others think of us)
- Virtue (living according to one's ideals)
- Power (the ability to control others)
- Bodily image (often equated with beauty and health)

Unfortunately, the locus of control for each of these criteria is external to oneself, thereby making self-esteem extremely fragile. Whenever the criteria by which one measures his or her self-esteem is external to the self, it will be vulnerable.

The Christian model for self-esteem is not based on such things as accomplishments and significance. Rather, as St. Paul proclaims when using his imagery of running the good race in 2 Timothy 4, the criteria upon which Christian leaders should judge themselves is trying our very best. Mother Theresa put it simply when she said that God had not called her to be successful but to be faithful.

Christian leaders who base their self-esteem on their faithfulness in attempting to live their Christian values and gospel imperatives will maintain a high level of self-esteem far more easily than those who look to externally controlled criteria.

We have interviewed Christian leaders in the marketplace who truly witness to others what it means to be a Christian leader. They identified three key values in their lives: to be filled with life, to be compassionate, and to be people of integrity. Leaders who are zealous and filled with life radiate a sense of joy and hope. They 'infect' others with these positive qualities. The word that was used most frequently by these individuals to encapsulate their values was the word compassion. They exuded compassion. Their most urgent concern was to use what gifts, talents, and resources God gave them to make the world a better place for others. Interestingly, the first ten people we interviewed, in six different regions of the United States, all described themselves as having 'to do the right thing, regardless of the consequences.' They were leaders who witnessed integrity in an extraordinary way.

We have identified six leadership principles related to the characteristic of self-definition that we will examine more closely in the remaining pages of this chapter.

1. Set boundaries.
2. Trust your gut.
3. Think in tenses.
4. Be comfortable with conflict.
5. Don't avoid the difficult.
6. Seek supervision and consultation.

Principle 1: *Set boundaries*

◇◇

All leaders, including pastoral leaders, have an ethical responsibility to set appropriate professional boundaries. Unfortunately, the media is filled with scandal headlines and stories of grave harm done to individuals when leaders violate these boundaries, or act inappropriately or immorally when boundaries are too permeable.

In order to ensure the safety and well being of patients, most medical schools require physicians to take a modern version of, or something similar to, the Hippocratic oath. This oath is a pledge of their commitment to do no harm whenever it is possible to avoid it and to work on behalf of the well-being of their patients. Leaders in ministry have a similar and sometimes a more powerful influence over those they lead because they can be perceived as the direct representative of God. Therefore, it might be appropriate to require all pastoral leaders to take a similar oath. Failure to keep that promise would be sufficient reason to remove someone from ministry.

Boundaries are the limits set by what is ethical for a person in a leadership position. They serve as a demarcation point. Any behavior that exceeds these boundaries is inappropriate. This is especially true when there is a violation of emotional, sexual, or genital boundaries by a leader who holds a differential of power.

Some Church leaders have trouble setting personal boundaries. They believe they are acting Christ-like when they set no restrictions on their availability to those they are serving. This is a misrepresentation of the Jesus portrayed in the gospels. Jesus often set limits even when faced with extremely needy individuals.

Four Reasons Why Boundaries Are Violated

Rationalization

Church leaders with a diminished sense of self-knowledge and self-awareness frequently rationalize inappropriate behavior. They attempt to justify what they have done, rather than to admit their inadequacies and are often able to commandeer an army of rational reasons for their behavior. Without adequate supervision or consultation, these leaders can perpetrate extreme harm, especially to individuals who have a strong or excessive need for the approval of their leaders.

Loneliness

Church leaders who are lonely or who have not developed their capacity for intimacy are vulnerable. They can manipulate others to inappropriately meet their needs for intimacy. Those who are in a milieu that fosters intimacy, such as spiritual direction and pastoral counseling, for example, must establish and keep very clear boundaries and communicate well-defined expectations for relationships with those they lead and work alongside.

Narcissism

As reported in a Fall 2000 *Human Development* article, 'Narcissism Sets Stage for Clergy Sexual Abuse,' by Paul Drucko and Marc Falenhain, professionals who cross sexual boundaries are often diagnosed as narcissists. Because of an inflated view of themselves, they do not feel compelled to restrict their behavior according to any societal norms. This attitude and consequent behavior are true in all areas of their lives, not just the sexual. They believe that they are exempt from the restrictions placed on 'ordinary' people.

Inattention to Transference and Counter-Transference

Transference and counter-transference are psychological phenomena that, if ignored by pastoral leaders, can lead to major problems in relationships between themselves and those to whom they minister. No one enters into any close, intense, helping relationship completely free from one's personal past. Transference is the phenomenon by which the follower projects onto the leader characteristics and traits that belong to some significant person in the past. Unconsciously, there is a hope that by acting out this scenario in the present, unfinished business with these significant others from the past will be resolved.

Counter-transference is the same phenomenon but with unresolved experiences of the leader being projected onto those being led. This is a convoluted process by which a leader projects onto those being led characteristics and traits of significant individuals from the past, often parental figures or siblings.

Both of these phenomena are unconscious, at least at the outset. The individuals involved are unaware that they are reacting to another, not as they are, but as they want the other to be. A particularly intense emotional reaction to the other is often a good indication that transference or counter-transference is present. There is a greater likelihood of transference and counter-transference occurring in more intense relationships, such as pastoral counseling, spiritual direction, formation work, or leading a parish.

Since the process of counter-transference is unconscious, it often requires the input of another—a peer, supervisor, or consultant—to help bring the phenomenon to consciousness. Even then, there will be resistance, since this forces the individual to deal with difficult and, at times, traumatic issues from the past.

Realize that these phenomena of transference and counter transference are asexual. Regardless of the sex of the significant person from the past, these emotions, hopes, and feelings can be projected onto a male or female in the present.

Negative Example

While in college a young woman entered therapy because of depression. Her therapist, a minister, would hug her and shared that his marriage was breaking up and how much he looked forward to the sessions with her. He called her to say that he had awoken at 3:00 a.m. experiencing a sense of guilt for not doing as much for her as he could.

Clearly, this was a situation in which the leader's own needs were propelling him into a violation of boundaries with a fragile, needy person. It was a situation that ended in confusion, pain, and destruction of trust for a young woman who had reached out to a professional for help and hope.

Positive Example

A formation director described his experience of working with a number of generous young men, individuals who came to religious life with the intention of giving themselves completely to God. On occasion, he found himself reacting intensely and inappropriately to some of them. There were individuals toward whom he had a strong negative reaction. He was unaware of any logical reason for this antipathy. There were other men in formation that he identified as 'outstanding' candidates, but found he had an inexplicable need to have them admire him.

The formation director consulted a wise older priest. They lived in the same community, so the older priest was not only hearing the director's version of what was transpiring, but was actually observing it. The older mentor was an astute, psychologically trained counselor. He demanded that the two of them spend time looking at the formation director's internal dynamics. On one occasion the mentor inquired about how much the director understood about the phenomena of transference and counter transference. The director said he saw his work as 'holy' not psychological. The mentor gently and patiently helped him come to an awareness of his counter-transference responses to the men. What could have been a negative experience eventually became a positive one because of the eventual realization of these dynamics of transference and counter-transference. As a result, the formation director set clearer boundaries in his relationship with the men he was leading.

Stop and Think

Are you aware of a time when you experienced a leader inappropriately crossing boundaries? What effect did it have on the individual or group being led?

Since transference and counter-transference are unconscious, it will take the assistance of another to help bring them to consciousness. Where do you get help keeping aware of and attending to your unfinished emotional business?

Are you aware of any time that you have been the recipient of someone else's transference? Did you react to their behavior? How would you like to respond differently in the future?

Principle 2: *Trust your gut*

◇◇

Listening is a key component of communication. When leaders are so literal and intent on 'active listening,' they may hear only the words spoken. While they may be able to repeat verbatim what the other has said, they may not have heard the real message that was conveyed. There is a distinction between listening and hearing. Hearing is a more complex process than listening. While listening attends to the words being spoken, hearing goes beyond the words and intuits the true message, that is, what is really being said. Overemphasis on listening only to words can preclude an ability to truly hear and understand the other.

Good listeners learn to listen at many levels. They hear the manifest content or the words being spoken. But they also go further and hear the latent content or the meaning behind the words. Sometimes this latent content is communicated at a subconscious level, with the speaker unaware of all that he or she is saying. Effective listeners are capable of hearing the message that is being communicated even when it is indirect or symbolic. Good listeners learn to listen with their heart and their 'gut' and not just their ears. They hear what is being communicated at many different levels.

When training leaders in communication skills, we encourage them to learn to listen beyond the words, attempting to hear the real message that is being conveyed. This form of listening occurs when listeners can emotionally distance themselves from the speaker and attend to their own emotions. When individuals experience high anxiety, they may have an unconscious fear of communicating their feelings directly, so emotions are communicated indirectly, often in a nonverbal, unconscious manner.

Therefore, when leaders can trust their gut—get in touch with the emotions that are transpiring within themselves—they often find clues to what the speaker is psychologically unable to communicate directly. The leader feels the message more than he or she hears it.

Jesse Rubin, a psychiatrist, hypothesizes a theory that he calls a 'matrix.' The matrix is the major emotion that an individual or group experiences. The matrix is communicated more often non-verbally than verbally. Leaders who spend time and energy focusing on their own feelings and listening to the manifest content indirectly, are often more capable of hearing the true essence of what is being communicated.

Effective leaders listen at many levels to: words and content, the latent content, symbolic language, and emotion as well as logic.

Frequently breakdowns in communication occur because leaders have listened so intently to the words being spoken that they miss the symbolic language that is being transmitted. An excellent example is our story of listening to a missionary from Ireland who asked, with tears in his eyes, if we knew what he missed most about his homeland. When he shared that what he missed most was 'a good potato,' our immediate, uncensored response was to laugh. However, we recalled the devastation caused by the potato famine in Ireland, a time when millions of people died and at least another million left Ireland never to see their families again. Realizing this fact, we were able to hear the pain that was being transmitted through the symbol of a potato.

Ordained and lay ministers alike are schooled in the value of religious symbols and the deep meanings they convey. However, this learning is often not readily transferred to the development of listening skills. Many Church leaders have been trained to think more than to feel, and getting in touch with one's 'gut' runs counter to this deeply ingrained proscription. This is particularly true when the leader is faced with a conundrum. We have observed how many Church leaders respond to pain with explanations and logic. The tendency is to treat heartache with an intellectual aspirin. Aspirins are for headaches, not heartaches.

Negative Example

A leader described a recent experience. He was asked to facilitate a staff that was described as a 'very difficult group.' The leader was anxious. The staff had recently attended a communication workshop where they learned techniques for 'active listening.' During the meeting they assiduously applied the technique of 'rephrasing' to avoid dealing with the anger and conflict that permeated the group. Rephrasing can be a valuable tool for growth; however, this staff was unconsciously using it as a defense against the anxiety of dealing with the difficult issues of anger and conflict.

Upon later reflection, the leader gradually came to the realization that his own fear of anger and conflict interfered with his ability to provide adequate facilitation. His anxiety caused him to focus obsessively on the content and the behavior that was observable. His facilitation could have been more beneficial to the group if he had been able to detach himself from the observable content and been aware of his feelings. It was only in supervision that he became aware of what was transpiring within. His own anxiety interfered with his ability to be in touch with his 'gut' and prevented him from truly hearing what was happening in the group.

Positive Example

During a pastoral counseling session, the client, who was usually rather reticent, became extremely verbose. The counselor strained to listen more intently. She became aware that, while the words were conveying one message, there seemed to be a more powerful, but less obvious message being communicated. She gradually realized that there were some powerful emotions being stirred within her. She disengaged from the words in order to become more aware of her own emotions and the significance of the emotions in relation to the client. She identified her primary emotion as anxiety, yet could think of no reason for the anxiety. This provided a clue that it was the client who was feeling anxious, but the anxiety was either not conscious or too fearful to discuss. By trusting her 'gut,' the therapist was able to focus on creating a climate in which the client felt comfortable enough to begin to acknowledge and explore his anxiety. This approach of utilizing one's feelings to help understand the other must be done gently and, often initially, indirectly.

Stop and Think

Can you allow yourself to 'feel' the communication by attending not only to the words, but also to what is being said through the silence, the symbolism, and the conveyed, unspoken emotions?

Can you recall a time when you really felt listened to, heard, and understood? What was there in the listening stance of the other that communicated this to you?

Are you as comfortable listening to your own emotions as you are applying logic?

Principle 3: *Think tenses*

During a workshop, while the participants were interacting, one of the team members leaned over and whispered, 'Think tenses!' Needless to say, we were confused. Later, we asked what he meant by that statement. The team member explained that it was important to listen carefully to the tenses that people used when speaking. He said that when people speak consistently in the present, past, or future tense, it conveys something about that person's life stance. This insight, which he later developed more fully, has influenced our understanding of leadership ever since.

Individuals often have a propensity toward focusing energy on one or another period of their lives, which an attentive leader can identify as the past, present, or the still-unfolding future. Where individuals choose to place their focus often reveals their stance toward life. When leaders comprehend this principle, they are in a better position to foster growth in themselves and others. Graphically, the principle looks like this:

When someone is always talking about **what was** in such a way that they convey an attitude of living in the past, it's possible that they may be prone to depression or the ill effects of deep regret. For example, a person may constantly speak of life as it was in the past, how he or she used to be, or experiences that happened 'back when.'

Those who are overly concerned about **what if** obsessively focus on the future. They have no control over the future and tend to live with a great deal of anxiety. Their mantra sounds like: 'What if I lose my job and cannot support myself,' or 'what if I fail at what I am doing?' Or someone may overly romanticize the future, thinking often in terms of 'If I just do this, then I'll have…' These individuals can miss the joy of the present and often leave loved ones feeling neglected or even abandoned.

There are two ways to live in the present. Some people tend to focus on ***what should be***. This can produce individuals who are often frustrated and angry. These individuals look at a situation and say: The country or the church should do such and such, or people should act in this way in a particular situation.

Lastly, there are individuals who focus on ***what is.*** They accept reality. This latter stance, ***what is,*** is usually indicative of healthy individuals who generally live in a relatively peaceful state. These people are able to integrate all four possibilities. While they commence from a stance of accepting the reality of what is, they can also look forward and backward. They can recall the past, learn from it, and bring that wisdom into the present. The past becomes a prologue of what can be. They can look to the future and see the possibilities. This stance also frees them to be prophetic people, challenging what should be. In their wisdom these individuals can find creative ways to integrate these various time elements into living with their reality as it is while cherishing the past and looking forward to the future.

Someone recently shared this helpful outlook with us: The past is history, the future is mystery, and the present is gift.

Negative Example

At a conference of Catholic school administrators we found ourselves at the luncheon table with one of the principals. Later we discussed the luncheon and discovered that neither of us had found the table conversation uplifting, and both of us had left the table feeling sad and somewhat depressed. It was then that we recalled the principle, think tenses. Revisiting the conversation we had with this educational leader, we realized that he was always speaking in the past tense. His conversation was peppered with endless comments about what was. He spoke of how much more the students applied themselves in the past. He followed this up with a series of related comments about the better quality of the teachers and school officials in the past. When we began to realize that his remarks were never about the present, or even the future, it became evident why we were feeling sad and depressed. Living in the past left him feeling depressed, and this emotion was communicated to us nonverbally. His nostalgic meandering cast a heavy pall on anyone in contact with him. We realized why many of the other principals at the conference had avoided his table.

Positive Example

Christian leaders are called to be life-filled and life-giving. We have had the privilege of working with a woman who epitomizes what this means. She exudes energy as well as a positive ambience, and this attracts others to her. Although she is a realist, she is a positive leader. In trying to understand why she is such a positive leader, we applied the criteria mentioned earlier to her conversations. We discovered that she identifies the reality of what exists in the Church and in the world today, both the positive and the negative. She rarely uses past tense, and when she does it is not to dwell morosely on what was. Rather, she reflects on the past as an opportunity to learn from it. She does not appear anxious over the uncertainty of what the future might hold. When she talks of the future, it tends to be with a prophetic voice, excited about the possibilities of what can be. Her reflections are generative and uplifting. She lives in the present, embracing the reality and accepting her limitations but never being overwhelmed by them.

Stop and Think

The next time you are in a group, listen to the predominant tenses used by different individuals. Can you perceive examples of the theory presented earlier?

Although it is more difficult, attempt to listen to yourself. Which of the four options would best describe you? Do you speak mostly about the past, the future, or the present?

If you tend to keep your comments about things in the present, is your basic stance one of being angry because things are not what they 'should be' or are you able to accept the reality of 'what is?'

As a leader how can you apply this principle?

Principle 4: *Be comfortable with conflict*

◇◇◇

There is a difference between being comfortable with conflict and seeking conflict. Healthy pastoral leaders, like all
healthy individuals, prefer to avoid conflict, but they overcome
their personal desire because they are convinced that avoidance of
conflict precludes success and growth. Conflict that is ignored or
avoided does not dispel or dissipate the conflict. Rather, it merely
forces the energy created by the conflict to assume a clandestine
expression that oozes out in inappropriate and destructive ways,
negatively affecting individuals and groups.

There are many ways in which leaders can help others become
more comfortable dealing with conflict. Here we address five:
helping people explore internal threats; modeling a willingness to
deal with conflict; modeling forgiveness; helping those involved
identify the real cause of a conflict; and responding rather than
reacting to behavior.

Leaders can help individuals or groups deal with conflict by
helping them explore what internal threats have produced the
need to enter into conflict. The major cause of conflict is threat
to self-esteem. It is this threat to self-esteem that often serves as
the catalyst that nudges individuals toward becoming embroiled
in conflict. Individuals can ascribe to very different theologies,
philosophies, or political realities. But it is not these kinds of differences, in themselves, that cause the conflict. Conflict usually
arises when the other person's beliefs challenge my perception of
myself—my self-esteem.

The second way to exhibit effective leadership is to model your
own willingness to engage in conflict and not avoid it. Conflict that

is dealt with and not avoided produces growth for the individuals and the group. Many people who avoid conflict do so because of their own fears, thus precluding growth.

When there is a disproportionate degree of anxiety in a group, the often-unspoken rallying cry, 'Kill the leader!' frequently emerges. Anxious individuals and groups engage in an unconscious or subconscious collusion to blame the leader for whatever threatens the group. This dynamic provides leaders with the opportunity to witness their personal beliefs about conflict. When leaders refuse to be intimidated by the conflict that is directed toward them, it helps to create a climate that demystifies the irrational fear of conflict. This can serve as a catalyst to invite the threatened individuals to acknowledge and dialogue about the perceived threat.

When leaders are attacked, they are provided with an opportunity to witness how anger and conflict can be resolved. Much of the current psychological literature on anger and conflict indicates that the treatment of choice for both anger and conflict is forgiveness. South African President Nelson Mandela witnessed this same wisdom when he proclaimed in his inauguration address that only mature leaders have the courage to forgive. Witnessing forgiveness in the midst of aggression and injustice is not the normal response and yet our violent world is in dire need of Christian leaders who can witness forgiveness in the face of conflict and hostility. As Alexander Pope said, 'To err is human. To forgive is divine.' Christian leaders are being called to be witnesses of the ultimate divine reaction.

The fourth valuable role that leaders play in managing and resolving conflict is to help those involved focus on the actual causes of the conflict, not the symbolic ones. Whenever there is an inordinate amount of energy focused on an inanimate object, such as money, buildings, church furnishings, etc., that energy is being dissipated on symbolic, rather than real issues. The cause of the conflict is never the inanimate object. These inanimate objects merely serve as lightning rods, attracting the intense energy that is probably related to some unmet or threatened need. In a later chapter we will develop the principle that behavior usually can be understood as addressing some human need.

The fifth recommendation is to respond, rather than react, to behavior. This principle is much easier said than done. When someone is hostile toward you, the normal reaction is to become defensive and react with hostility. Hostility breeds hostility. This contagion of hostility precludes dialogue and prevents change. Effective leadership involves emotionally withdrawing from the conflictual situation when it erupts. The challenge is to learn to move from an immediate heart response, responding solely from emotion. The task is to use your head, your cognitive skills, before allowing any response to escape from the mouth. It may be necessary to withdraw physically from an ego-threatening situation in order to attain such emotional detachment. Allowing oneself time for this emotional maneuver puts you in a position of responding, rather than reacting. Again, this is often much more difficult to achieve than it sounds.

Research on Catholic Church leaders indicates that clergy, members of religious congregations, and lay ministers all have difficulty in dealing with conflict. Given the fact that the research covers all the major players, it is not difficult to see the need for growth in this area so that our leaders can be pastorally effective.

Negative Example

Various members of a parish described a problem that was destroying the morale of the community. There was intense conflict within the choir. Individuals had chosen 'sides,' and the conflict had become a public scandal. As often happens in such situations, the sides had become antagonistic, not only toward each other, but also toward the choir director for not siding with either group. The pastor, fearful of conflict, simply tried to avoid dealing with the toxic situation. The conflict continued to escalate, and the choir director eventually left. She was replaced by another director, who inherited the problem and also left after a very short tenure.

Positive Example

We facilitated a meeting in a parish that was riddled with conflict. Two individuals were identified as the leaders of the opposing factions, and we were warned against putting these two individuals in the same discussion group. By a twist of fate, the two conflicting parties ended up in the same group. Rather than be cowed by their seemingly intense hatred of each other, we pressed them to explore the true genesis of the conflict. Initially, they focused on a disagreement that had existed over the ownership of property that went back several generations. Continued probing revealed that they were really unsure of why the conflict existed. As a result, dialog began and, hopefully, healing was initiated.

Stop and Think

Can you think of a recent situation where conflict emerged? How did you respond?

If a similar situation were to present itself, how would you respond differently?

Which of the five identified roles for effective leadership do you personally need to address?

Where have you acquired the skills of dealing more
effectively with conflict?

Principle 5: *Avoid niceness*

◇◇◇

O ne word that might describe many pastoral leaders or
Church leaders is 'nice.' Niceness, at times, appears to be
an endemic quality of these individuals. The question you may
be raising is 'what's wrong with being nice?' On the one hand,
there is nothing wrong with being nice. However, niceness can
be a characteristic that is detrimental to effective leadership. This
principle of avoiding niceness is closely related to the previous
principle of being comfortable with and embracing the growth
that comes with healthy conflict.

When David Nygren and Miriam Ukeritis undertook their
1990s study of the future of religious life in the United States
(FORUS), they included one aspect that helped to explore a
rarely examined dimension of religious leaders. They asked congregations to nominate their 'most caring member.' An eminent
researcher from Boston College, David McClellan, administered
tests to these caring members. Among his results was one very
interesting fact: These caring members scored in the ninety-third
percentile on a scale called 'niceness.' When questioned whether
this should be worrisome, his response was an unequivocal
'definitely!'

David went on to describe how these 'nice' people avoided anything dealing with anger, conflict, or confrontation. As a result, he concluded, they would make very poor leaders. Effective leaders must be comfortable and deal with these sometimes-troublesome dynamics, or stagnation results. We are not advocating that Christian leaders be unkind. Rather, we encourage an exploration of the reasons why too many Church leaders evolve into the epitome of niceness. We suspect that it is at least partially related to their fear of anger, hostility, conflict, and confrontation.

In the previous principle, we alluded to research indicating that many ministers are fearful of conflict. While the Nygren/Ukeritis study focused on members of religious congregations, research on priests and on lay ministers sponsored by the United States Conference of Catholic Bishops and the National Pastoral Life Center discovered that the fear of conflict, anger, and hostility sometimes resulted in Catholic leaders who hid behind a veil of niceness to avoid these difficult and painful emotions and situations.

A number of years ago we conducted a research project in which we interviewed business professionals who lived their lives in such a way that they truly witnessed to others what it means to be a Christian leader. We dubbed these individuals 'wisdom people.' The major characteristic that defined them was integrity. After probing the values of the wisdom people, as well as who or what influenced the development of those values, we asked, 'Where do you experience stress in living those values?' Being people of integrity with a need to do the right thing often put them in conflict with others. Yet, most of the subjects had a difficult time identifying stress in their lives. One area of stress that did emerge was the tension between being successful while being faithful to their Christian ideals.

Some of these individuals equated being a good Christian with being nice, in a shallow, saccharine-sweet way. On a daily basis they made tough, painful decisions in order to see their businesses succeed. These choices sometimes placed them into an internal conflict because they did not perceive themselves as 'nice' in doing this. It sometimes produced guilt. The essence of being a good Christian leader is not being nice, but rather doing the right thing. Jesus probably would have been described by his contemporaries as many things; we doubt that 'nice' would lead the list.

Negative Example

An organization had just elected a new leader. They had been through some painful, conflictual, and difficult times in the few years prior to the election. Things had been improving but they were not yet out of the woods. One of the candidates for leadership presented himself to the group as a gentle, non-confrontational peacemaker. Swayed by this self-portrayal, the group overwhelmingly elected him. The group got what it wanted, not necessarily what they needed. The new leader was truly gentle and non-confrontational, but such a one-dimensional leadership style does not foster growth. Sometimes groups elect the leaders they think they want, not necessarily the leaders they need.

While working in a therapeutic community in a psychiatric hospital we witnessed a similar phenomenon. At each community meeting the patients elected the chairperson for the next meeting. One day they elected a catatonic patient, who never talked and stood rigidly in the corner for hours on end, sometimes being burned by the cigarette that he passively held in his hand. At that time there was a great deal of tension on the ward. If addressed, the tension could have produced positive results. The patients, fearful of the tension, elected a chairperson who was sure to do nothing, someone who was nice.

Positive Example

The business manager of a parish shared a concern. The parish had made a commitment to become more collaborative. They were convinced that God was calling them to do so and that they would be more effective in fostering the mission of Jesus if they became more collaborative. Most of the staff was attempting to grow as a collaborative team. However, one staff member was either unwilling or unable to do this. While consulting with us, the business manger came to the realization that the staff member was impeding the mission. Initially, he was reluctant to fire her because some members of the parish would be offended by the idea of the parish firing someone. It was not the nice thing to do. Ultimately, the business manager did the right thing, however, and fired her.

Stop and Think

Do you know people who are 'too' nice? What is it that causes you to label them as such? How effective are they as Christian leaders?

Think of a group to which you belong. What criteria did the group use for choosing its last leader?

Can you think of an example of a leader who balances niceness and integrity?

Principle 6: *Seek supervision and consultation*

<<<<<<<<<<<<<<<<<<<<<<<<<<<<<<<<<<<<<<<<<<<<<<<<<<<<<<<<<<<<<<<<<<

Current business leadership literature encourages leaders to have a mentor or coach. Whether that person is called coach, mentor, supervisor, or consultant, the principle is the same: Leaders need others to give them feedback and to help guide them through the difficult maze of leadership. There is an adage that says a lawyer who has himself or herself as a client has a fool for a client. The same could be said of leadership. The leader who never seeks the advice or counsel of another is foolish and will be ineffective. Every leader needs another both to provide insights and to help in avoiding self-deception.

The presence of an objective other can have many beneficial results. Such a relationship can lead to greater self-knowledge, while the absence of such an objective person could result in self-deception or rationalization.

Our group leadership training demanded participation in a supervisory group. The thought of participating in a session that left us open to criticism and evaluation produced anxiety. The anxiety triggered contrasting fantasies. On the one hand, the supervisors heaped praise and adulation on us. On the other hand, the fantasy had us being dismissed from the program because of our incompetence. Neither fantasy became reality. The supervision session was, at times, extremely painful and difficult because it forced us to honestly confront our inadequacies. However, supervision also proved to be the greatest source of growth. Through supervision and subsequent consultation, we acquired an honest appraisal of our strengths and weaknesses. Supervision and consultation with wise, probing, honest practitioners provided the data that fostered our development as leaders.

During the training we discussed with another trainee, a psychiatrist, how to benefit most from the supervision. Her answer was, 'Bring whatever you find most embarrassing to supervision.' That proved to be invaluable advice. No one enters into a leadership role without personal 'blind spots.' Every leader brings into the present situation their 'unfinished business' from the past. Unless those blind spots and unfinished personal development issues are brought to awareness, they seriously impede the ability to develop as a successful leader.

It has been our observation that only the most mature leaders take advantage of supervision and consultation. Immature leaders are too fearful of exposing their inadequacies to others. When they fail to avail themselves of these resources, they not only shortchange themselves, but, more importantly, they do a disservice to those whom they profess to lead. All leaders can benefit from coaches, mentors, supervisors, and consultants to help unearth whatever interferes with developing leadership skills more fully.

Some leaders have discovered the advantage of using a peer group for supervision and consultation. Among the many benefits of peer supervision is the ability to tap into the wisdom, experience, and resources of other leaders who grapple with similar issues. Another value is that the members of the group can challenge each other when they settle for simplistic solutions to complex issues.

Negative Example

A psychologist recounted his experience of establishing a supervision group for the ministry formation personnel in his local area. The psychologist informed us that he had observed very little growth and progress among the formation directors over the course of the group. He concluded that the reason was that the directors were unwilling to honestly reveal their shortcomings to their peers. They were a group of women and men with a strong need to impress others and unwilling to look at their inadequacies. If they had the courage to face their inadequacies, they could have become more effective in their formational ministry leadership.

Positive Example

A woman who was a leader of a large diocesan agency shared that when she was first employed by the agency, she was blessed to have as her immediate supervisor a wise woman who had worked in the field for more than twenty-five years. The leader told us of the generosity of the woman in freely imparting wisdom accumulated through decades of successes and failures. The new leader's openness to learning from this genuine ministerial supervision allowed her to utilize the knowledge of the other.

Stop and Think

Do you have a consultant/supervisor, mentor, or peer support group? How honest and open are you within this group?

What are some of the areas where you feel a sense of inadequacy as a leader? Have you shared those areas with your supervisor or consultant? If not, why not?

Have you ever been a consultant, coach, supervisor, or mentor to another? If so, what did you learn from that situation that might be helpful to you and to others?

The Discerning Leader

◇◇◇

Church leaders should be guided by one question—the discernment question: 'Where and how is God calling?' This is true for leadership of both individuals and groups. Certain prerequisites are necessary to begin a process of discernment. First, the leader must be a person of prayer. Before entering into any discernment process, adequate time must be given to reflection and prayer. The second prerequisite for developing a discerning attitude is to strive for and work toward an internal freedom. There is a relationship between these two prerequisites. The leader's prayer should be focused on discovering those aspects of the self that interfere with the ability to be completely open to where God is leading.

As mentioned in chapter 1, leaders of national church organizations for whom we conducted a retreat day were forced to reassess their spirituality and prayer lives because their administrative ministry was quite distinct from their former more interpersonal, direct-care pastoral ministries. Prayer must fit one's unique situation.

In contrast to these leaders, we recall working with another group of leaders, a pastoral council. This group functioned like many parish councils of old, a body of corporate management. We shared our belief that a pastoral council is primarily engaged in discerning the will of God for the parish community. With this task as a background, we encouraged them to spend at least a quarter of their meeting time in prayer, reflection, and study. How is it possible to discern God's will without spending time in prayer? They, in turn, informed us that they had no intention of engaging in anything more than a cursory opening prayer. They were there to make decisions, not to pray. We have often wondered what happened to that council.

St. Theresa of Avila offers one very clear criterion to discern if someone is a prayerful person or not. This clear criterion is that person's growth as a compassionate person. Prayerful, discerning leaders are compassionate leaders.

The second prerequisite for becoming a more discerning leader is to continue to seek an inner freedom from one's own wants and needs, which might prevent you from being attentive to God's will. As mentioned in the discussion of principle 6, such freedom is only possible when leaders are willing to allow another, such as a supervisor, consultant, or spiritual director, to enter into the personal space that influences your decisions.

In this chapter, we will explore seven areas in which leaders are called to develop a discerning heart and the capacity to lead from what they discover in their discernment.

- The freedom to change one's approach as the situation changes
- The desire and capacity of the other(s) to change
- The developmental readiness for change

- How to assume a facilitating, rather than a dominating role
- When to 'feed' and when to 'frustrate'
- The multiplicity of reasons for behavior
- The present developmental stage of the other

Principle 7: *Act like a chameleon*

Some say that when the Greek Republic was in decline, the Athenians asked Demosthenes, the great orator and statesman, for advice. The sage simply replied, 'Do not do what you are now doing.' The response probably confused the questioners, but its logic is profound. Whatever the Athenians were doing was not working. Therefore, his advice was both simple and profound: cease to do what is not working and try something else.

Chameleons are fascinating creatures to watch. They intrigue by their ability to change colors to adapt to their surroundings. A brown chameleon that was clinging to the trunk of a tree just a few minutes before has now transformed into a vivid green to blend with the leaves on which he is now perched. Demosthenes had the wisdom to value the need for change. The chameleon has been given the natural ability to adapt to the situation. Leaders do not have an innate ability to change. They must decide, like Demosthenes, that it is the wise choice.

Some leaders tend to be rigid in their approach to every situation, even when each situation calls for a unique response. Effective, mature leadership involves assessing the situation and adapting one's style. The leadership style and approach must fit the unique situation. The principle is a simple one: Change your approach to fit the situation. Don't be rigid. This is not advocating that leaders adopt a 'wishy-washy' approach. Rather, it suggests changing and adapting one's approach when necessary for the sake of the mission. Failure to adapt limits pastoral and leadership effectiveness.

Some leaders, who have adopted a one-dimensional approach to leadership, are either too rigid or have become so enamored of a single approach that they are unable to consider options and alternatives. At a recent meeting a leader described the agenda for the evening. He declared that each item could be addressed by applying the same approach. He was unable to look at a variety of theories or options. Leaders who are one-dimensional are ineffective in the complex world in which they must operate. Good leadership requires the ability to think and act broadly, to discern which principle or principles apply in a given situation. Effective leaders often discover that their initial discernment was inaccurate and there is a need to try a different direction.

We trained under a wise priest-psychiatrist who believed that many ministers, especially those formed in the pre-Vatican II Church, have a tendency toward obsessive-compulsive thinking and acting. He believed that what is necessary for effective leadership today requires the ability to be extremely flexible and adaptable. He sympathizes with those who are obsessive-compulsive, knowing how difficult it is for them to make the adjustment.

Negative Example

An immigrant priest had been a very effective and dearly loved pastor in his own country. There his brusque behavior was perceived as concern, care, and love for his people. He had been appreciated and loved. His new parish was largely Spanish speaking like the previous one, yet the two cultures were very different. He experienced a great deal of tension and stress as pastor in the new place. For two years he continued with his brusque approach and managed to alienate the majority of parishioners. He knew he was ineffective but was unable to change his approach for one that might be more pastorally effective. As a result, he was transferred and felt as though he had been a failure. He was equally ineffective in subsequent parish assignments. His rigidity and inability to change was his downfall.

This case is not an isolated one. We have often seen Church leaders move from one ministry to another and attempt to apply what worked in a previous situation without any discernment about whether it would be appropriate and effective in the new place.

Positive Example

Without doubt, one of the most positive examples of someone who had the wisdom and fortitude to adapt and change was Archbishop Oscar Romero, the martyr of El Salvador, an admired and revered pastoral leader of the twentieth century. The story of Archbishop Romero is well known. As a younger member of the hierarchy he seemed more concerned about those with influence, wealth, and power. But a chance encounter with a group of poor, oppressed people transformed him. He ceased to minister from a position of privilege and power and came to realize that his pastoral leadership and effectiveness demanded a true conversion, a turning away from one approach to another.

Romero discovered that to be pastorally effective he had to shed whatever separated him from the people he was called to lead and embrace his own vulnerability. In the archbishop's life we can see the wise leader who was able to change and adapt, not only because he knew it would make him more effective, but more importantly, because it was the right thing to do. He chose integrity. In his case the ability to change and adapt was a key step in his process of conversion.

Stop and Think

Think about two individuals whom you are in a position to lead. Can you delineate what approaches might be helpful with each one? What approaches would be unsuccessful? What approaches would be disastrous?

Have you ever been the recipient of pastoral ministry from someone who was unable to connect with you? Could the approach the person was taking with you have been effective with someone else? What might characterize that person?

Can you identify a pastoral encounter where you believe you were ineffective? Were you attempting to utilize an approach that had been effective in a different situation? What might you have done differently in order to be more effective?

Principle 8: *Assess the desire and capacity of the other to change*

◇◇

There are two preconditions for personal change to occur. The person must have both the desire and the capacity for change. Frustration will occur when a leader fails to acknowledge the necessity of both these preconditions.

A participant at a workshop presented the case study of a 'difficult person' with whom she was dealing. The participant had tried a variety of approaches in dealing with this person but nothing worked. Her frustration was evident as she pleaded with the presenters for some additional ways to approach the problem. One of the members of the workshop team offered a number of excellent recommendations. Another member of the team indicated that there were two questions to be asked before applying the excellent suggestions that were just offered. Does the other person want to change? Does that person have the capacity to change? Trying to change another or help another to change before addressing these two questions almost guarantees ensuing frustration for the leader. Even when there is a desire to change, there may not be the capacity to change, either because of a lingering pathology or because a lack of psychological development militates against the change.

After reflecting on these two questions, leaders need to acknowledge that they are limited in what they can achieve. They are not responsible for change or the lack of it in others. All that leaders can do is assist others in finding solutions for their problems. It is the person with the problem who determines whether or not change will occur.

It is important to note that not everyone wants to change even when they seem to indicate their desire to do so. Even though their behavior may create problems and havoc for others, they may be very content with themselves and their situation. At times, even problematic behavior is preferred to change, since the person involved is more comfortable with the known than the unknown. The individual may not really want to change, because change is disorienting and often perceived as less attractive than staying with what is familiar.

There is a greater sense of hope when the problem is lack of capacity, rather than lack of desire to change. When there is truly a desire for change, the leader is in a position to assist the other in locating resources to help in the journey toward growth and maturity. The skills necessary to make significant changes in one's behavior patterns can be learned with good coaching and determination.

Negative Example

A parish staff member was consistently disruptive. The disruptive member was controlling, and frequently undermined whatever attempts were made by the rest of the staff to minister more effectively. Other staff members described in great detail what they had done to change the problematic and offensive behavior of the disruptive member. They had sought advice from an outside resource and were given a number of techniques to use, none of which accomplished any change. As a result, the frustration and anger toward the 'difficult person' increased. Because of the intensity that they were displaying, we suspected that this might be a case of scapegoating, finding someone to blame for their lack of progress and success.

We finally met the offending individual. In our discussions it became apparent that she was psychologically underdeveloped and was incapable of being a contributing member of the staff until she had achieved a greater maturity. In addition, she was perfectly satisfied with herself and her behavior and saw no need to change. As long as the staff continued in their determination to change her, they were doomed to failure and frustration because she simply lacked both the will and the capacity to change.

Positive Example

A principal reported an experience she had with a first-year teacher. During the first three months of the school year, the principal had received a number of complaints about this young teacher. The principal shared these parental concerns and complaints on a number of occasions with the teacher. Still the complaints continued. The principal decided not only to share the concerns but to listen to the teacher. Initially, the teacher was defensive, but the principal did not react to the defensiveness. In time, the teacher began to express disappointment with herself. Her goal in life was to be a teacher. She had worked diligently in college and achieved high grades. She mastered the content of her coursework. Her weakness was in the practical application of the theory.

The principal was convinced that this first-year teacher had both the desire and the potential to be a good educator. The principal offered her the opportunity to be mentored by one of the school's more experienced faculty members. She gladly accepted the offer, and the complaints began to lessen and eventually stopped altogether.

Stop and Think

Picture a time when someone tried to change you. Were they successful? What was your reaction? What happened to the relationship?

Think of someone whom you would label a 'difficult' or 'problem' person. Have you ever tried to change him or her? Can you assess your success or lack of it based on whether or not the other both wanted to change and could change?

Before you try to assist someone to grow, ask yourself the following question: As far as I can tell, do they have both a desire and the capacity to change?

Principle 9: *Think developmentally*

◇◇◇

Both individuals and groups grow in a developmental way, progressing through predictable stages. Erik Erikson's theory of human development is described as epigenetic—that is, each stage builds upon the previous ones. Erikson's model, beginning with trust and culminating with integrity, encompasses a lifetime of development and is a slow process. This model and adaptations of it have formed the basis for much of the understanding of how individuals grow. Erikson shows how individuals have the ability to choose between two poles at each level of development. People either grow toward maturity or become fixated or regress at each level. They tend to regress if they feel overly challenged by the task of the next level of growth. Failure to build one stage upon the other results in a psychologically underdeveloped person or a dysfunctional group.

The goal of a leader is to foster a climate and process that facilitates individuals and groups to function at a generative level. Generative people focus on others rather than on themselves. They are the compassionate ministers whose primary question is

'What gifts has God given me and how can I use them for others?' This generative attitude was the primary characteristic of individuals we dubbed 'wisdom people' in our earlier research. These were leaders in the marketplace whom we interviewed. They were effective leaders because they were perceived as being generative by those they lead. They were perceived as compassionate leaders whose primary concern was the welfare of those they served.

Helping people grow toward full maturity and generativity involves two distinct steps. The first step is to assess the developmental stage, the level at which a person is functioning in her or his growth toward maturity. The second step is to set a climate that is conducive to growth. In church organizations there is often an expectation and a hope that every minister will be functioning at the level of generativity. This is unrealistic. Ministers, similar to the general population, are in various stages of evolving toward full maturity. Expecting a person to function at a generative level when they have not proceeded through the earlier stages of development leads to frustration and failure. Sometimes religious ideals of perfection do not allow for the slow process of development. For instance, until a person develops his or her sense of identity and the capacity for true intimacy, consistent generativity is impossible. He or she may be capable of performing individual generative acts but has not yet acquired the capacity for sustained generativity. This unrealistic expectation must be checked in a particularly careful way when a leader is working with youth. Most youth only have the capacity to do 'random acts of kindness.' They are usually not yet at a point of true generative capacity—they just don't have it in them.

This same assessment and climate-setting process is true for working with groups as well as individuals. Groups, like individuals, develop sequentially through stages. Effective group leadership involves being able to identify the stage at which the group is functioning in order to help move it to the next stage of development. Many leaders are trained to work with individuals, but their formation has lacked the equivalent training in understanding group stages and dynamics. Effective group leaders have a theoretical developmental model that they can apply to the groups with whom they are working. Such a model allows for successfully facilitating the group towards its mission and goals.

A Negative Example

A formation director in a religious congregation had an idealistic, almost obsessive-compulsive, personality. Perfection was the norm by which he evaluated himself. Not surprisingly, it was also the norm he used to judge each of the men in formation. He assiduously studied the congregational documents and used the idealism and perfectionism inherent in them as his norm for judging the men in formation. Nothing less than perfection was acceptable. He did not acknowledge the reality that each candidate was at a different level in his process of psychological development. As a result, he failed to help the candidates set realistic goals. Because of the unrealistic expectations placed on them, most of the candidates left the formation program. Many of those who stayed experienced major crises early in their religious life because they had not built the developmental foundation that would have helped sustain them. They had developed a pseudo-perfectionist attitude and foundered when they discovered that they were far from perfect.

A Positive Example

We know a priest who is perceived by most of his parishioners to be an outstanding pastor. He meets regularly with the staff. During these sessions he often takes a few moments to assess the psychological development of the staff person. When he is aware of the fact that the lack of development is interfering with the pastoral effectiveness of the person, he will directly address the issue. After dialogue, he will offer opportunities, at the parish's expense, for the person to attend programs that will assist them in their growth. The pastor knows that the investment will reap great benefits for the parish. One of the side benefits has been that there has been virtually no changeover among the staff in years.

Stop and Think

Envision an individual with whom you are working. Can you identify the level of psychological maturity at which this person is operating? Do you know what you would do to help her/him move to the next level of development?

Visualize a group with whom you are working. Are you able to identify the level of group development at which they are operating? What might you do to create a climate that would encourage their growth to the next level?

Do you have concrete models of individual and group development from which you work? For example is there a conceptual framework, such as the Erikson model, that influences your work with individuals? Do you have a similar model for evaluating groups? We have described one such model in our book, *Building Community: Christian, Caring, Vital.*

Principle 10: *Facilitate, don't dominate*

◇◇

One mantra for a pastoral leader is 'never do for others what they can do for themselves.' In other words, *facilitate: don't dominate*. This principle, which sounds so simple, is often a stumbling block for those in helping roles such as ministers, care-givers, and pastoral leaders. Those who work with others who are especially vulnerable, such as the very young, the very old, and the infirm, are particularly prone to doing too much for the people whom they serve. It is often disrespectful and an affront to human dignity to do for others what they are capable of doing for themselves.

There are a number of reasons why leaders fall prey to over-stepping boundaries and providing care to those who are capable of taking care of themselves: 1) the action responds to a need in the helper, 2) there is a misperception of need, 3) the helper is try-ing to maintain a sense of superiority, and 4) simple arrogance.

One area where it is most difficult to see the potential in the other is when someone we know and love begins to experience diminishment, as with aging or poor health. A common response to watching a loved one struggle with simple activities is to pre-maturely rush in and do for them what they are capable of doing for themselves. This response can be an unconscious attempt to allay one's own discomfort and feelings of helplessness rather than a genuine response to the needs of the other. I experienced this when my then ninety-two-year-old mother lost her sight. I found myself rushing in too frequently to assist her with simple tasks that had become more difficult for her. She ultimately convinced me that she was capable of doing much more than I allowed her to do. I had to learn to become more patient because my over-helping wasn't really helping her. Rather, I was allaying my own pain at seeing her grow old and frail. When we are more overly solicitous and protective of people than is required, we too easily contribute to their deterioration.

The model for implementing this principle of not doing for others what they can do for themselves is Jesus Christ. Through-out the gospels Jesus is revealed as a caring, compassionate person, one who constantly saw gift and potential in others that was evident to only a few. He took a motley group of fishermen, prostitutes, tax collectors, and outcasts and challenged them to do what few before or since have done because he saw and respected their potential.

At times, refusing to do for others what they can do for them-selves is a very simple act. When attending a children's Mass at a parish, we were fascinated watching a second-grade boy valiantly, but unsuccessfully, trying to light the Easter candle. The prob-lem was a simple one: He was too short to reach the wick. We watched a teacher approach and wondered what she would do. It was evident that the children in the pews were getting antsy waiting for Mass to begin. We had visions of her taking the taper from the child and lighting the candle herself. Instead, she tipped the candle and let the boy light it. An act that was simple but meaningful. It was not just this single, isolated act that impressed us. Not only did the children do all the readings at the Mass, but also one young child played the piano, while the music teacher stood behind him turning the pages. We would not be surprised to return to this parish in a decade or two and discover a vibrant faith community, with these children having grown up to take responsibility for its leadership.

While facilitating a discussion among parishioners in a small, rural parish, we asked them what they needed. One of the participants responded, 'another Sister Mary.' When pressed to expound on that comment, she informed us that the parish had recently lost a pastoral minister, Sister Mary, who had ministered there for a decade. She did everything: ran the choir; served as the lector at Mass; led all the parish meetings; ran the religious education programs; and was the chairperson of the pastoral council. When she left, nearly all activity in the parish ceased. Many people might have looked at her and praised her for the zeal and devotion to the parish. We would be much more condemnatory. The major criterion for discerning your effectiveness is how many individuals have you empowered to assume leadership for what you have been hired to do. We wish we could say that 'Sister Mary' is an isolated case, but the opposite is true. She may be more the rule than the exception.

A Negative Example

A former provincial of a religious congregation recounted an experience to us. The General Council of the province had made money available to members to initiate self-help programs for the poor. One group, working in a developing country, among extremely poor people, indicated that the people would be incapable of taking the leadership for any project. As a result, the funds were diverted to a non-church group in the same area who believed in the capacity of the poor to assume leadership. And they did.

A Positive Example

A social justice minister told us that as a child her family lived in poverty. She also said that she used to have very little confidence in herself. She attributed her transformation from insecurity to confidence to a pastor who asked her to take a leadership role in the parish. She immediately informed him that she was incapable of doing what he had asked. His response was, 'Have you ever tried to do it? And, if not, how do you know you can't?' His belief in her gave her the encouragement to overcome what she described as an 'an introverted personality' and take the risk of assuming a role of leadership. She credits this man with the significant change that occurred in her. He believed in her and her leadership capacity and did not take her refusal without challenging her own beliefs about herself. It might have been 'easier' for him to assume the leadership of the project himself, but he is a man who not only believes in the capacity of others, but whose actions give credence to that belief.

Stop and Think

Do you believe that most individuals have the resources within themselves to solve their own problems? In your ministry, how do you specifically communicate this belief?

Can you identify someone for whom you are constantly 'doing'? What about this person or about you leads you to do more than is necessary? Can you narrow the reasons to one of the four we mentioned earlier? How can you change the pattern?

Since need-enhancing behavior is usually unconscious, whom do you utilize as a consultant or supervisor to help you attain greater self-awareness?

Principle 11: *Feed and frustrate*

◇◇

A sound principle for church leaders is to feed and frustrate. This principle can be applied to both individual and group leadership, and is closely related to principle 12. Some leaders provide too much direction and help for those with whom they are working, and in a sense 'overfeed' them. This can result in the person getting help developing a sense of inadequacy and/or dependency. Other leaders provide too little direction and help, causing frustration, apathy, and often anger.

The essence of this principle is to find a balance between these two actions. Wise leaders have an almost innate ability to know when they have been over-feeding. They are willing to cause frustration by withholding their input in order to force others to rely on their own insights, talents, and abilities. Leaders need to realize that when they do not respond to every need, anger will result. Effective leaders develop a sense of when it is appropriate to feed and when it is appropriate to frustrate. Developing this balance results from a combination of experience, feedback, and, often, supervision.

There are at least three ways that church leaders nurture and feed. First is focusing on the giftedness they see in others. This can run contrary to an attitude that has been fostered in the past— focusing on what was wrong or defective. Many were trained to be 'fixers' rather than animators. Focusing on strengths produces many more positive results. In a society that is more prone to criticism than affirmation, the surprise of being affirmed can be disarming and transforming. The leader has a choice: focus on strengths and health or weaknesses and pathology.

The second manner in which leaders feed others is by affirming people for who they are, not just for what they do. Affirming people only for what they do often propels people to become super-doers, leading to burnout. Affirming the qualities in others helps to form a positive alliance that creates an atmosphere conducive to dialogue, growth, and creative productivity.

When working in Australia we heard that Australians often describe themselves as knockers. They subscribe to what they refer to as the 'tall poppy syndrome.' If one flower, or one person, or one group rises above the others, you knock it down. Australians may claim this as characteristic of their culture, but we have observed this same phenomenon in many of the cultures where we have worked.

A third way to nurture and feed is to validate the feelings of the other. Validation does not imply agreeing, or even completely understanding. However, validating the feelings of another both acknowledges the appropriateness of those feelings and provides an opportunity to further explore those feelings without fear of judgment or condemnation. Feelings, of course, are neither positive nor negative. They are pleasant or painful. Feelings are simply an emotional reaction to some internal or external stimulus. The new catechism of the Catholic Church acknowledges that feeling and passions are morally neutral. Therefore, acknowledging and validating the feelings of another helps to erode the negative connotation associated with having certain feelings.

A Negative Example

A leader bragged about how she did everything for the individuals for whom she was responsible. In reality, she had a terrible fear of conflict and confrontation and believed that by taking care of everything for others, she could avoid conflict. Needless to say, she was a very ineffective leader. She fostered dependency rather than independence. Her tendency to over-feed negatively affected her ability to be a good leader.

A Positive Example

While conducting a conference for Catholic educational leaders in Australia we included a gift-discernment process as part of the training. Weeks later, as we visited one of the schools we were approached by the principal, who informed us that he had made a decision after the conference. In the middle of each day he chose to stand in front of his office and reflect on the gifts he saw in his teachers as they walked by. He would then call them over and share his thoughts with them. When asked what the result was, he said, 'It has begun to transform our school.' The teachers began to tell the other teachers and staff the gifts they saw in each other. In turn, the teachers began to share the gifts they saw in their students. The principal's leadership style of affirming gifts has had many positive repercussions throughout the entire school.

Stop and Think

Are you aware of times when you have tended to err on the side of either too much feeding or too much frustrating in your leadership position? Are you aware of why that occurred? How would you do it differently in the future?

Can you recall a time when someone spontaneously affirmed the gifts he or she saw in you? What effect did that have on you?

Are you aware of a time when someone validated your feelings? What effect did that have on you? Are there certain feelings and emotions that you find particularly difficult to acknowledge within yourself? Are there feelings that produce a sense of guilt or shame when you acknowledge them in yourself?

Principle 12: *Consider multiple causes and multiple responses*

◇◇◇

Life would be relatively simple if each action caused a consistent and predictable reaction. This, of course, is not the case. People are not laboratory experiments, and it is impossible to predict the cause of a particular behavior simply by observing the reaction. Behavior is multi-causal.

For instance, you observe someone who is extremely controlling. There is no way to accurately predict what causes the controlling behavior through simple observation. The single observable behavior of control might be caused by any of the following: a threat to self-esteem, fear, greed, lack of psychological development, or any one of a number of other causes. It could also be caused by a combination of these factors. One behavior that is frequently misinterpreted is silence. Some presume that they can almost miraculously intuit the cause of silence in another, but in reality, a number of emotions might produce silence: fright, fear, awe, confusion, boredom, or a myriad of other possibilities.

All we see is the behavior. The cause lies beyond our observable perceptions.

Just as behavior is multi-causal, so also, one cannot accurately predict resultant behavior based on knowledge of the cause. Effective leaders learn that even when they know the cause, they cannot with any consistent accuracy predict what the response will be. A person who is threatened might react in a number of different ways: withdrawal, aggression, arrogance, defensiveness, submissiveness, humor, etc. Human behavior is complex and does not lend itself to overly simplistic rules. Effective leaders are those who understand this complexity and do not presume they can discern the cause based on the behavior, nor predict what behavior will ensue based on a specific cause. Often what interferes with embracing this principle is an excessive dependency on one's experience: 'I remember seeing this same situation in my last position. I remember that the cause was . . . . I took this action and it worked. Therefore, I'll do the same thing again.' Each situation is unique, involving different people and different circumstances and requires responses that are discerned in light of those realities. The secret is to always think 'multi' and avoid making simplistic conclusions based on past experiences.

A Negative Example

We were teaching a course on anger. At the very beginning of the class one student entered the room, turned his chair away from the front of the room, and with his back to us, faced the rear wall. In addition, he pulled out a crossword book and for the entire two hours of the class assiduously worked on crossword puzzles, seemingly oblivious to us and the content we were teaching.

Our reaction was predictable and simplistic as we immediately labeled this behavior as a sign of disrespect. The longer we witnessed this 'disrespect,' the angrier we became. Our beliefs produce our emotions and, in this case, we were generating a *large* dose of anger.

After class, the crossword puzzler came to see us and explained that throughout his life he had an enormous fear of anger. With almost heroic strength he decided to attend the class and forced himself to stay and listen to what we said. He was extremely fearful of facing his anger. His behavior in the class did not result from disrespect but from fear. Our presumption about the cause of his behavior had interfered with our ability to be more compassionate leaders.

A Positive Example

An elderly sister worked in a parish as a pastoral minister—a position she had previously held in two other parishes. She was a joy to observe. Often faced with difficult and conflictual situations and people, she possessed a unique gift of discerning and responding to each situation and person seemingly without any preconceived notions.

A teenage boy had covered the parish hall with graffiti. Some staff immediately blamed it on his 'dysfunctional family' (always a safe and easy target). Others were convinced that it was a disrespectful, hostile act. They attributed it to the disrespect often shown by 'those people,' a designation ascribed to individuals from certain cultures. But this sister refrained from making any initial judgment even though she had seen similar behavior from teens both in her current and previous parishes. She suspended judgment until she had a chance to meet with him. Upon meeting with him, she simply asked him why he had painted the walls. He beamed and informed her that he had noticed how barren the room looked and decided to use his artistic abilities to add some color and life to the room. He was equally proud of the fact that he had used his own money to buy the paint. It was evident to the sister that he fully expected to be praised for taking the initiative. For another teenager, the painting may have been an act of hostility, but for this young man it was a positive act of creativity and generosity.

Stop and Think

Have you ever been with others in a situation that was potentially dangerous? Did everyone react the same way? Can you visualize the myriad ways in which people reacted to the same situation? Can you see how this reflects the principle, 'consider multiple causes and responses'?

Picture times when you have been angry. Can you identify the many different reasons that produced this emotion?

Develop a greater capacity for thinking more broadly. The next time you are in a leadership role, focus on the other and ask yourself, 'What are some of the reasons why he or she may have done this?'

Principle 13: *Think needs*

Human behavior often has its origin in addressing and meeting human needs. If you wish to understand a person or group's behavior, you need to consider what human needs are being met by that behavior. Accepting this leadership principle helps to make sense out of your own and others' at times seemingly erratic behavior.

Needs are something that God places in human beings to propel them toward wholeness and holiness. They are internal drives that motivate individuals toward growth. Needs are more than just desires. An individual might desire to develop a deep personal relationship with a particular individual. That might never occur, and the person would continue to function and grow. In contrast, it would be a serious psychological deprivation to be totally isolated and alienated from all human beings. There is a basic human need to belong to someone or some ones. When needs are not satisfied, people become sick and die. That death could be spiritual, physical, and/or emotional. As noted psychologist Abraham Maslow asserted, human beings have a limited number of needs, such as the need to survive, to maintain safety and security, to belong, to be loved, and to maintain one's self-esteem. These basic needs, though few, are powerful motivators.

Behaviors that seem erratic, illogical, or self-defeating can be understood only when one accepts that at some level these behaviors are meeting human needs. This drive-oriented mechanism is usually unconscious. When you observe behavior that defies any logical explanation, contemplate what need the behavior might be meeting in the other person. For example, might the behavior be meeting the need to feel safe and secure or the need to feel good about oneself or protect oneself from rejection? Often, the normal reaction for many people, including leaders, when confronted with erratic behavior is to react rather than respond in a helpful way (recall principle 4 on dealing with conflict). The challenge is not only to refrain from reacting, but, more importantly, to move to the level of cognition and try to understand the need that produced the behavior. It is this cognitive leap that often provides the opportunity to make better leadership decisions and, ultimately, to make a helpful response to the other.

It is essential for leaders to operate from a basic understanding of human needs as motivating drives. Maslow's hierarchy of needs that we mentioned earlier is one helpful model for identifying these. There are certainly others, but what is key is to embrace some model and utilize it when examining behaviors in light of needs.

A Negative Example

A young woman sat next to me on a flight. She was nasty to all the cabin staff, and I found myself negatively judging and labeling her. I found myself avoiding her, which is perfectly acceptable behavior on an airplane flight. I withdrew into some reading material, attempting to avoid her as much as possible. About thirty minutes into the flight, she turned toward me with a smile and declared, 'Now I feel comfortable!' She explained that she had a terror of flying and the behavior I observed was a reaction to that terror. Her need was to feel safe. Her behavior was merely a manifestation of that need. I had judged her by her behavior and failed to perceive her behavior as merely an expression of a need.

A Positive Example

I worked with youth in an after-school program. One of the group workers sent a thirteen-year-old girl to see me. The worker said that she was behaving in a very aggressive way toward the other girls in the group. It was my responsibility 'to solve' this problem. At the time I was absorbed with some other problems. My immediate reaction was to send this teenager home and tell her she could come back when she had learned how to behave—clearly a reaction. Instead, I allowed God's grace to intervene and, instead of sending her home, asked her if she had eaten lunch—a potentially helpful response. She informed me that she didn't like the 'slop' they served at school. I then asked what she had for breakfast. She replied, 'I never eat breakfast.' Suddenly aware that I was absorbed in a reactive mode, I shifted gears and inquired when she had last eaten. She began crying. As the tears began to dissipate she told me that they had no food at home or enough money to pay for her school lunch. She hadn't eaten in three days. Only then did I realize that she was not having a most important need met—food. She was hungry. It was this hunger that produced her behavior.

Stop and Think

Recall a time when others were confused by your behavior. Are you aware, now, of what needs you may have been trying to address by that behavior?

Consider the behavior of another that you have found inexplicable. Think needs. What need might have influenced that behavior?

Tasks, Functions, Roles, and Skills of Principled Ministry

◇◇◇

L eaders are more than idea people: They must be action people. For leaders to be successful, they need to be able to imple-
ment their dreams. Even 'natural born leaders' need to develop
the skills to see dreams and ideas become specific, lived realities.
For instance, in the past, religious congregations appointed individual members to be in charge of formation programs without
providing the training needed in those positions. Fortunately, in
most cases, this has changed. Yet, some dioceses and religious
congregations continue, even up to the present, to appoint pastors
and other key leaders without providing adequate training for
these positions. This is especially problematic when those positions are people-related and not merely task-oriented roles.

While there have been significant strides made in providing people with one-on-one skills through field education placements and clinical pastoral education, there still seems to be a dearth of adequate training in working with groups and communities. Today, much pastoral ministry involves leading groups, which is far more complex than leading individuals. Groups and communities have the power to be life-giving or life-draining. This is especially true in parishes. When leaders understand the complex dynamics of groups and develop skills to work with these dynamics in helpful ways, their leadership will be much more productive.

The next eight principles focus on some of the skills and functions of pastoral leadership of both individuals and groups. In this chapter, we explore such issues as:

- Understanding the role that ambiguity plays in creating tension, stress, and conflict
- Creating a climate that is conducive to growth through dialogue
- Exploring the basic elements involved in the skill of confrontation: directness, gentleness, and consistency
- Learning the value of avoiding triangulation, thereby facilitating rather than impeding growth
- Utilizing collaboration as a major method for effective leadership
- Learning to deal with difficult people more effectively
- Realizing that as Gospel people we are called to growth, never to mere survival

Principle 14: *Avoid ambiguity*

◇◇

Ambiguity produces stress, anxiety, and conflict. The normal reaction to the anxiety, for both individuals and groups, is to incorporate defenses. The unconscious goal of any defense is to reduce anxiety. When an individual or group is in a highly defensive stance, it usually interferes with the ability to listen, to hear, and, ultimately, to grow. Therefore, it is apparent that one of the tasks of leaders is to clarify whatever is unclear or ambiguous.

General Rules for Clarifying Ambiguity

- Recognize that ambiguity is especially problematic in intense helping leadership relationships such as spiritual direction or pastoral counseling.
- Ask penetrating, probing questions.
- Clarify the purpose.
- Establish clear expectations regarding confidentiality.

Many, if not most, church leaders function as a spiritual director or pastoral counselor, at least at times. Clarification is especially important in such roles, and leaders have an ethical responsibility to carefully clarify expectations and measurable goals. Failure to do so can result in a prolonged, manipulative, dependent relationship. Often, pastoral counselors and spiritual directors, because they are seen as God's agents, have the potential to do harm to those they are leading. The leader's goals for these kinds of meetings should be articulated simply and directly, free of jargon and ambiguity. Clear purposes provide criteria by which all parties involved can evaluate growth and progress toward a stated goal.

One of the most effective methods for removing ambiguity across a wide array of leadership situations is to provide information. An even more effective method is to ask probing, perceptive questions. Posing appropriate questions provides an opportunity for everyone involved to obtain greater clarity and thereby reduce anxiety. Information, data, or advice cannot be absorbed when anxiety is very high. Attempting to appeal to the mind when the emotions are in ascendancy is often counterproductive. Effective leaders ask more questions than they provide answers.

In supervising group leaders, we came to the realization that when groups fail, it is most often because the leader has failed to clarify the purpose of the group. The frustration that many experience in groups can be attributed to the fact that the group has not articulated a clear, realistic, and shared purpose. Without clarity the group meanders, without any tangible results to show for its efforts. As you can imagine, this produces frustration. Stephen Covey describes the need for clarity of purpose in his *Seven Habits of Highly Effective People* when he counsels leaders to begin with the end in view. One specific way in which pastoral leaders can assist those with whom they work is by helping them establish clarity regarding their mission. Individuals and groups are more likely to be successful if they have articulated a statement of mission.

The issue of confidentiality demands clarity in every leadership situation, and it is the responsibility of the leader to raise the issue. Never assume that all parties involved share the same or even similar understandings of the meaning and expectations regarding confidentiality. This is an area where the expectations need to be stated clearly by the leader and explicit agreement articulated by the individual or group being lead. This requires dialogue about what each person—including the leader—involved understands by confidentiality and its implications in this particular situation.

Negative Example

The secret to avoiding ambiguity is to ask clarifying questions without assuming the role of a 'Grand Inquisitor.' We were facilitating a meeting a few years ago and during a meal, sat next to one of the participants. He began asking 'clarifying' questions of everyone at the table in a way that appeared accusatory and left people feeling and reacting defensively. This inquisitor's seemingly probing, clarifying questions were perceived as hostile, alienating all those at the table. The way in which the clarification is sought is at least as important as the seeking of the clarification.

Positive Example

In contrast to the previous example, we were privileged to study group counseling under a very wise and insightful psychiatrist. On one occasion we were selected to present a tape of a session for supervision. The psychiatrist was uncanny. Not knowing that the tape was six weeks old, he began to hypothesize about what might happen with the group in the future. We listened in awe. His predictions were an historical accounting of what had transpired in the group during the five weeks since the tape was made! With great anticipation we became a client in one of his therapy groups. Initially, we were terribly disappointed. We expected him to make brilliant interventions. Instead, he consistently summarized and asked clarifying questions. It took awhile for us to realize that this is the primary characteristic of good leaders and therapists. They don't make brilliant interventions; they ask penetrating questions that help the participants clarify the issues for themselves. The psychiatrist's clarifying questions and gentle probing conveyed a concern and desire to know more about the individual and was never perceived as inappropriate and never evoked a defensive reaction.

Stop and Think

Can you remember a time when you experienced ambiguity about a task you were asked to tackle? How did you feel during that time? What helped to clarify the ambiguity? What effect did the clarification have on you?

Think of an individual or group with whom you are working. Can you clearly articulate the purpose? Is that purpose clear, realistic, and shared? Do you revisit that purpose on occasion to help focus and evaluate progress?

When you are in a leadership role, do you establish clear expectations regarding confidentiality? How do you accomplish this clarity?

Principle 15: *Create a climate that fosters dialogue*

The late Father Philip Murnion, founder and former executive director of the National Pastoral Life Center, worked closely with many bishops and had developed excellent relationships with them. The day before he died he wrote to every bishop in the United States. He stated that he wanted to pass on one word of advice: 'Dialogue, dialogue, dialogue!'

We recently concluded a project interviewing the oldest retired archbishops in the United States. While gathered at the University of Notre Dame in Indiana to review the results of the individual interviews, the discussion focused on changing Church structures. One of the archbishops interrupted the discussion to say that we were focusing on the wrong issue. He stated that if people would dialogue, they would build trust. If they built trust, they would develop relationships. And, if they developed relationships, probably there would not be such a need to focus on structures!

Attitudes and Behaviors That Foster a Positive Climate for Dialogue

- Develop a safe climate.
- Communicate a desire to know and understand the other.
- Keep the focus on the other, rather than on oneself.

One of the tasks of leaders is to create a safe climate, a climate of trust where individuals are open to both listening to others and to sharing their own thoughts, ideas, and emotions. Dialogue helps build relationships that contribute to growth and mission. The United States Conference of Catholic Bishops (USCCB) identifies the four calls of every Christian in a short, prophetic document titled *Called and Gifted for the Third Millennium*. The first three are the calls to holiness, community, and ministry/mission. The fourth is a call to Christian maturity. In that document the word most frequently used to describe the mature Christian is 'dialogue.'

A safe climate is a trusting one that encourages a sharing of the truth. Leaders must guard against something called 'groupthink.' This occurs when the members of the group are more concerned with pleasing the leader or maintaining positive relationships among themselves than in making the best decision. Leaders need to challenge groups to speak the truth, sharing their honest opinions and concerns, regardless of the consequences. Unless there is a common search for truth—to the degree that it can be discerned—decisions made will be seriously flawed.

Some ways in which a leader helps to create a safe environment are by challenging any belittling of others; establishing an explicit oral contract about mutual expectations; and ensuring clear expectations regarding confidentiality.

The second way in which leaders help to foster dialogue is by communicating a desire to know and understand the other. One way to accomplish this is by being present to the other. Being present implies the ability to put everything else aside and to give one's full and undivided attention to another. Once present to the other, leaders should focus all their energy and attention toward trying to understand what it must be like for the other, and to communicate that desire to understand. Sometimes leaders may not be able to fully understand others or their positions, but communicating the desire to do so helps establish a climate that is conducive to dialogue.

The third major task of leaders in creating a positive climate for dialogue is to keep the focus on the other, not on oneself. Some leaders tend toward a narcissism that is evidenced by their self-referent response to whatever is being discussed. Effective leaders keep the focus on the other, never on themselves. The more that the leader reverts to sharing their experiences, the less likely will the listeners be convinced that there is a concern for them.

Listen with attention to how people respond to one another. Someone, for instance, might say, 'I just had a wonderful vacation in Ireland.' Inevitably, some will immediately begin talking about their previous vacations in Ireland. Others will ask questions to encourage the speaker to explore the personal reasons why the vacation was so wonderful. Obviously, it is the second group that is communicating their interest in the other.

Leaders who use their own experience as the norm for understanding others impede dialogue. These are the leaders whose common response is, 'I know just how you feel.' They use their own experience as the primary norm for understanding the attitudes and behaviors of the other. They interpret all behavior from the limited and biased scope of their own experience.

A Negative Example

An elderly religious sister apologized for not sharing during a meeting. She recounted an experience as a young member of her community. Her first superior was a woman whom she described as 'arrogant and cantankerous.' She described a situation that occurred about two years after she was assigned to this particular convent when she had shared an insight about improving the quality of communal life. The superior immediately responded, 'No one cares what you think!' The sister who was recounting the story commented that as a result of that single experience she had developed a belief that her opinions were not valued. Consequently, she rarely spoke at meetings.

A Positive Example

Cardinal Walter Kasper recently addressed a meeting of the Catholic Common Ground Initiative. He emphasized the need for dialogue and respect for the other. He said that since the Second Vatican Council, 'dialogue has become a fundamental expression and feature of

Catholicism.' As president of the Pontifical Council for Promoting Christian Unity, he is in constant dialogue with leaders of other faith traditions. Cardinal Kasper acknowledged that his approach in speaking with another is to look first for areas of agreement, and then to 'let the disagreements surface.' He respects the dignity, integrity, and freedom of the other. He identified the Christ of the gospels as the only true model for Christian leadership. Jesus claimed not only to have the truth, but also to be the truth (Jn 14:6), yet he came among his disciples 'as one who serves' (Lk 22:27).

Stop and Think

Recall a time when you experienced a climate where you felt safe enough to share beyond a surface level. Can you recall who or what helped to create that climate?

How does it help build a relationship when the other communicates the desire to listen, hear, and understand? Conversely, what effect does it have when you do not feel understood by the other?

Recall a time when you were sharing a personal experience and the listener responded by informing you that because she or he had had a similar experience, he or she understood exactly what you meant. Did you feel listened to, heard, and understood at that time? Can you suggest a different response?

Principle 16: *Be direct, gentle, and consistent*

◇◇◇

Effective leaders are direct, gentle, and consistent. Many Christian leaders tend to be strong in one of these areas and weak in the others. It is the presence of all three that usually produces positive outcomes. One of these qualities without the other two leads to ineffectiveness. Leaders, however, should never expect themselves to be perfect in any or all of these qualities. The realistic goal is to continue to become stronger in each of them.

We have met many helpers who were extremely gentle. Gentleness is a very positive quality and an attribute of many helping people. Sometimes, gentleness and niceness are erroneously considered synonymous. As mentioned in our discussion of principle 5, David McClellan in the FORUS study identified an extremely large percentage of members of religious life as being 'nice.' Dr. McClellan indicated that this attribute, by itself, was not as positive as it might sound. Gentleness is usually a positive quality, whereas niceness is often a negative aspect of leadership.

By contrast, there are leaders who are extremely direct, but direct to the point of hostile aggressiveness—the opposite of gentleness. Their approach often produces defensive fear in the persons whom they are attempting to lead. However, it appears that more religious helpers have trouble being direct than being gentle. At times, it appears that indirectness is almost endemic among ministers.

When individuals can combine gentleness and directness with the quality of consistency, they are usually effective leaders. Consistent individuals are not prone to vast mood swings and there is certain predictability about them. They generally deal with all individuals in a consistent manner, avoiding overt prejudices. They are also consistent in their dealings with each individual in ways that are fair and objective. Their decisions are not made on capricious or subjective criteria, but rather on principles and values that have been communicated clearly to those they lead.

One of the best leaders we have ever encountered was a Jesuit psychiatrist, James Gill. We had the opportunity to observe Dr. Gill in both a leadership and helping role on numerous occasions. Each occasion was a primary learning experience, as he was one of the gentlest people we have ever encountered. However, his gentleness was always tempered with an honesty that was courageously direct, eschewing any 'political correctness.' He exhibited a predictable consistency, treating each person with respect.

A Negative Example

A female faculty member shared how she had been treated unfairly and ultimately forced out of her position. She said that even those who supported her would not stand up for her. We listened to her tale and felt her pain. When asked what she intended to do, she indicated that she was returning to the school for an anniversary and intended to tell the people who had been so cruel to her how angry she was with them. When we next met her, we asked how the event had gone. She said it went well. We then inquired whether she had confronted those who had been so cruel and unjust to her. She proclaimed vehemently that she had let them know how she felt about them and the treatment that she had received. When pressed to describe what she said, she informed us that she had sent them a note after the celebration. When asked about the contents of the note, she stated, 'I thanked them for all they had done for me.' At this point she could see our confusion and informed us that the thank-you note was written on the back of a picture of St. Sebastian, a picture of his martyrdom with dozens of arrows impaling his body! This is the epitome of indirectness.

A Positive Example

A staff related how they felt victimized by one member, Sara, who monopolized all conversations and controlled all meetings. As we observed the interactions of the staff, it became evident that Sara indeed monopolized the conversations, but the rest of the staff did nothing to challenge her behavior. It was the passivity of the staff that allowed Sara to dominate. Finally, one of the members of the staff quietly turned toward Sara and said gently, 'Thank you, Sara. We have heard your thoughts on the subject. Let's now hear from the others.' Sara sat quietly and listened to the others. We had the impression that she was relieved. It appeared that she did not know how to set limits on herself and needed someone to apply the brakes when she was out of control. She was confronted gently and directly, and the group had a productive meeting.

Stop and Think

Recall a time when you felt a responsibility to share something that would be difficult for the other to hear. Can you recall and evaluate how direct you were?

Were you also able to say what you believed in a way that communicated concern and care for the other?

If you believe you were weak in either of these two dimensions, can you identify what fears or expectations may have influenced your weakness?

Principle 17: *Model and challenge*

L eaders are concerned with influencing and motivating others to grow. The psychologist Abraham Maslow suggested a
simple model for achieving this. His recommendation is that leaders should concentrate on two fundamental tasks—modeling and
challenging.

Sometimes leaders work with individuals and groups who
appear to have become stagnant or even moribund. The physics
principle that 'bodies at rest tend to remain at rest' holds here. No
movement or growth is likely to occur unless there is an external
force to motivate that change. The leader is capable of initiating
that change by challenging the individual or individuals to movement and growth. That challenge, however, will be ineffective
unless leaders model the behavior that they are advocating. When
there is a gap between the modeling and the challenging, those
being led are less likely to place any credence in what is being
suggested.

St. Francis of Assisi is reputed to have said, 'Preach the gospel .
. . and sometimes use words.' Francis was a leader who continues
to influence generations of people. He lived what he preached
and therefore was a credible witness.

Pope John Paul II was a leader who witnessed the need to
challenge and model. We attended an audience with him shortly
before he died and were touched by his physical frailty. As we
walked past him, we were aware of his trembling hands and
stooped demeanor and realized that he must have been painfully
aware of his profound diminishment during his later years. Most
of his major talks and letters during his last years were peppered
with a recurring message—the importance of forgiveness and

reconciliation. A poignant picture of Pope John Paul II appeared on the cover of *Time* magazine in 1984. It showed the pope bending toward Agca, the man who shot him. The pope visited him in jail to model what he so eloquently preached, the need for forgiveness and reconciliation. His moral authority as a leader, like every other leader, is commensurate with his willingness to model what he preached.

Of course, the ultimate leader is Jesus. The New Testament is filled with stories of how Jesus modeled this role of leader as someone who both challenged and modeled. These inspired writings are replete with stories of Jesus calling those who listened to new life. The people of Galilee came *en masse* to listen to this itinerant preacher. They heard his parables of healing and forgiveness, and watched him heal those who suffered. They heard his challenge to be compassionate, and they observed the compassion he exhibited toward those who were in pain and marginalized.

As mentioned earlier, most behavior is directed toward addressing some human need. When leaders fail to challenge, they probably do so because it meets some need within them, such as the need to be accepted or loved. When they fail to model what they challenge others to, they lose all credibility.

A Negative Example

While visiting a patient in the coronary care unit of a hospital, we overheard a doctor pleading with the patient in the next bed to stop smoking. The patient, a survivor of a heart attack, listened attentively as the doctor passionately and convincingly lectured on the potentially lethal effect that smoking could have on the patient. We were impressed how this medical leader lovingly and compassionately challenged the patient. However, as we left the hospital, the first thing we observed was a doctor, still wearing his surgical greens, puffing on a cigarette! Thankfully, the patient did not witness what we did.

A Positive Example

One of the great theologians of the last century was Karl Barth. There is a story that one of his fellow professors was surprised that a person as intelligent as Barth believed in Christ's resurrection and asked him how he could possibly believe in such a thing. Rather than to try to impress the colleague with his exceptional theological mind, Barth's answer was, to say the least, unexpected. He simply responded, 'Because my mother told me so!' Barth's mother was a person who witnessed to him. She lived her life as a profound declaration of her belief in the resurrection. It was the witness of her life, more than all the compelling theological arguments, that convinced Barth.

Stop and Think

Who are the leaders in your life who have been most influential? Are they individuals who modeled and challenged? How does their behavior influence the way you lead?

Visualize an individual or group that you are trying to influence as a leader. Apply the two criteria of modeling and challenging to the situation. What behavior are you attempting to change? Is there is anything that is interfering with your ability to challenge the other? How do they witness you as modeling what you are advocating?

What is your favorite passage in the scripture that depicts
Jesus as someone who both challenged and modeled?

Principle 18: *Avoid triangulation*

◇◇

Triangulation is a dynamic that exists when two individuals
or groups are in conflict and refuse to deal directly with the
other. In an attempt to resolve the conflict, one of the individuals
or groups tries to involve a third party, usually a leader, thus creating a triangle, two against one. Triangulation usually heightens the
conflict and rarely, if ever, results in a satisfactory resolution. The
alienated party accurately perceives that an injustice has occurred
through the allegiance of the leader with the other, and the anger
intensifies. Any time leaders allow themselves to be manipulated
into a triangled situation, they eschew the very growth that they
are attempting to facilitate.

Visually, it looks like this. Person or group A has a conflict with
B. Rather than deal directly with each other, one of the parties
involves C, often the leader. If the leader succumbs to this manip-
ulation, the isolated party experiences a sense of injustice.

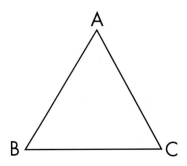

Leaders have a number of helpful options when approached with a situation that could result in triangulation. They can take the role of a coach, a consultant, or a supervisor. For example, the leader might meet with the involved individuals or groups and assist them in communicating directly with each another. The leader could facilitate the communication by helping to clarify, especially through the use of insightful questions. The role of the leader is to create a climate where people can be heard and understood. Whatever helps to facilitate that climate is a valuable contribution.

When triangulation is evident, the goal of the leader is to create a positive climate for dialogue, not to resolve the conflict. To be effective, he or she must refuse to be manipulated into siding with one or the other party, keeping in mind that it is the responsibility of the parties in conflict to resolve it in an appropriate and helpful manner.

A hospital administrator had a tendency to become triangulated. She knew it was ineffective but continued to be manipulated into that position. She was an insightful person who knew what was transpiring, but continued to be sucked into the triangle. She had a great need to be liked by others and achieved personal satisfaction by being perceived as a 'savior. ' When leaders allow themselves to be triangled, it is usually because the other has tapped into a vulnerability or need of that leader. As mentioned earlier, most behavior is need-directed. Knowing one's vulnerabilities and needs is the best way to avoid being manipulated into a triangled situation. People with low self-esteem are particularly vulnerable to being triangled. This is especially true when one's criterion for self-esteem is significance or being liked by all.

There is a subtle form of triangulation that frequently occurs that does not involve the classic triangulation of two individuals or groups. Rather, individuals sometimes attempt to triangle leaders into assuming responsibility for issues that are clearly not the leader's problem. For instance, an irresponsible individual faced with a deadline will attempt to manipulate the leader into taking action to allay the problem. When leaders are manipulated into rushing in to fill vacuums and voids that are created by others, they are being triangled. A primary principle of leaders should be, 'Never let another's problem become your problem.' Leaders must not resolve problems when they are the result of a lack of planning by the other.

A Negative Example

A youth minister in a parish related the following story to us. She was a recent college graduate who had been approached by the pastor to assume the role of full-time, paid youth minister of the parish. Reluctantly, she agreed to do so. Inwardly, she felt insecure and unprepared for such a role. For the two years that she was a staff member she found herself being triangled on a regular basis. Frequently, during disputes and conflicts among parish staff members, she felt herself drawn in by one or the other of the conflicted parties. Because of her insecurity she had an excessive need to be valued by the other, older staff members. Therefore, she would often side with whoever seemed to carry the most influence in the parish. She also found herself regularly being triangled into conflicts between the youth with whom she was working and their parents. When the youth would approach her with complaints about the parents, she would side with the youth in the hope that such behavior would make her more acceptable to them. Needless to say, she was completely ineffective and managed to alienate almost everyone in the parish.

A Positive Example

During one of our meetings with the staff of a parish that is seen by others as a model of vitality, we mentioned the concept of triangulation. The staff immediately grasped both the concept and the subtle ways in which it did and could influence their ability to continue being a vital parish. Each of them talked about instances and situations where they allowed themselves to be manipulated into triangulation. At a subsequent meeting, they reintroduced the topic of triangulation and began applying the principle to what was occurring among them as a staff. They were honest and perceptive in identifying where triangulation was occurring in their staff dynamics. This was a mature group that was able to confront personal weaknesses with honesty and humor. Having identified some of the areas where triangulation was occurring, they committed themselves, as a staff, to confront its emergence in themselves and in each other whenever they discovered it in the future.

Stop and Think

Are you aware of a time when you involved another in triangulation? How was the situation resolved? What long-term effects did resolving the situation through triangulation have on your relationship with the other parties?

Have others tried to triangle you, as a leader, into their conflict? Were you manipulated into being triangled? If so, what was the need or vulnerability in you that allowed this to happen?

Can you identify some of the more subtle ways in which triangulation occurs in your relationships and groups?

Principle 19: *Collaborate*

◇◇◇

We had the opportunity to offer a presentation to the staff of the neonatal unit of a large urban hospital. Before accepting the invitation, we asked the medical director of the unit what topics he wanted addressed. His response was a single word, 'collaboration.' When asked why he chose this topic, he explained that if the medical, clerical, cleaning, and social service staff did not collaborate, babies could die!

The response was both challenging and thought provoking. We found ourselves asking whether the lack of collaboration in church institutions might lead to spiritual death. Fortunately, many church leaders have come to realize that collaboration is more than just a good idea; it is absolutely essential for mission effectiveness.

An architect, a student in a course on collaboration, was asked why he was convinced that collaboration was important. He responded, 'If I don't collaborate with the construction people, the electricians, the plumbers, and everyone else, my family wouldn't eat.' There are a number of reasons why collaboration is an important principle for leaders. The two examples mentioned earlier offer practical reasons.

Collaboration, as we have described it in a previous work, is the identification, release, and union of all the gifts present within the community/organization in ministry for the sake of mission. The key issues are three—gift, ministry, and mission.

GIFT ⇨ MINISTRY ⇨ MISSION

Effective leaders are characterized by their ability to animate the gifts of others, which is at the heart of collaboration. They also foster structures that facilitate collaboration. The major focus of collaborative leaders is to bring together the differing gifts of all to accomplish the mission of the organization. Church leaders who are collaborative begin from a common vision. The vision and mission of the Church is to be an evangelizing community, bringing the Good News into every segment of society. Collaboration is the primary means for doing this.

A collaborative style of leadership is required for the complexity of issues faced by leaders in our time. Collaboration proceeds from the conviction that no one person has all the answers or all the gifts. Rather, the gifts of all are necessary to accomplish that mission. It is the responsibility of the leader to assure that processes are in place that allow for the identification of the gifts of all involved.

In a 2000 address to the Oblates of St. Joseph, Pope John Paul II wrote that in order to accomplish its evangelizing mission of bringing the Gospel into every segment of society, it is imperative that Church leaders become more collaborative:

> In order to meet the contemporary demands
> of evangelization, the collaboration of the laity is
> becoming more and more indispensable. This is a
> new, unprecedented opportunity that God is offer-
> ing us.
>
> **—John Paul II**
> **February 17, 2000**

Other Church leaders have also challenged others to greater collaboration. Cardinal Roger Mahony of Los Angeles, for example, in his pastoral on parish, *As I Have Done for You*, writes that parish (and other) leaders will be effective to the degree that they become 'more collaborative and inclusive.'

It is not only religious leaders who advocate the need for collaborative leadership. In *Mastering the Art of Creative Collaboration*, business leader Robert Hargrove writes:

> The inspiration leaders of the future will be
> those who can draw from the vast diversity of
> people with different specialties and allow their
> seeming disparate perspectives to interact, collide,
> and germinate into truly unique and creative ideas.
> The ideas drawn from creative collaboration will
> change the way we view . . . the world.

It is fascinating to compare the language used by Hargrove in describing the business leaders of the future. It parallels the language often used by religious leaders. He talks about the business world being involved in a shift 'to an era of reconciliation, an era of compassion' in order to solve the chaotic problems of the twenty-first century. Hargrove is convinced that the transformation of the workplace will be the result of 'an expanded concept of what it means to be a human.' His conclusion is that this new entity will be 'a collaborative person.'

A Negative Example

A community leader considered herself an excellent collaborative leader. She spoke frequently to others with great pride about her leadership skills. But she assumed direct responsibility for everything and never tapped the gifts of her members. She was so convinced of her sterling characteristics as a leader that she became very controlling and made all decisions unilaterally. In no way did her words reflect her actions. The members of her community painted a very different picture of her than the one she had of herself. In fact, behind her back, the other members would joke about 'their great collaborative leader.'

A Positive Example

An educational leader often spent time reflecting on the gifts of the faculty and staff and informing them of the gifts she recognized in them. Her behavior and affirmation of their gifts resulted in a contagion of spontaneous gift-affirming among the faculty and staff. Each month they celebrated the birthdays of their peers and would take time to both pray for and affirm the gifts of those celebrating birthdays. A culture of giftedness emerged, and this culture manifested itself in the life of the school community, especially during the centenary celebration of the school. Everyone was involved in both the planning and execution of the celebration. Each person's gifts (faculty, staff, and students) were acknowledged, and everyone was invited to a role based on his or her gifts.

Stop and Think

What criteria do I use to evaluate myself as a collaborative leader?

Can I identify specific ways in which I see collaboration in my ministry?

Am I aware of times when collaboration has not worked? Do I know why it didn't?

Principle 20: *Learn to deal with difficult people*

◇◇

We have received an increasing number of requests for leadership workshops on dealing with difficult people. The requests raise a question for us. Who determines who the 'difficult person' is? Sometimes, the difficult person is the one so labeled by the leader, and sometimes it is the leader who is the problem and truly difficult person. We offer here two tools for dealing with difficult people—multiple causality and multiple lenses.

Multiple causality is a principle asserting that each behavior has many causes. It is impossible to determine the cause of the behavior exclusively by observation. For instance, a person may be difficult because they have a mental illness, a pathology that causes disruptive behavior. The same problematic behavior, though, may have its genesis in some other cause. One possibility is a lack of adequate psychological development, or an attempt to work though some 'unfinished 'relationship or issues from the past. The only thing of which we can be certain is that the behavior of the other creates a problem for the leader. The cause is often a mystery. The more we enter into dialogue with the other, the more likely we are to understand what might be causing the behavior. Assuming we know the cause simply from observing the behavior will lead to false conclusions.

We will be most effective in understanding difficult people if we can view the behavior through a variety of 'lenses.' There are at least three specific lenses we would recommend.

- The behavior is the result of a problem in the other.
- The behavior stems from a relational problem between you and the other.
- The behavior is a problem in the group dynamic that is being manifested through a single individual.

The problem can be any of the multiple individual causes enumerated. Often, the problem is as simple as the fact that the other person is truly a problem.

However, the problem may be a relational one, especially if you are the only person who sees the other as difficult. If that is the case, it may take a third party, such as a consultant, supervisor, or insightful peer, to help you, as leader, identify why you are having problems with this person. Perhaps there is something toxic in the relationship between you, and it will require understanding and change on the part of both parties to resolve the problem. When the problem is a relational one, it may be the leader who is the problem. Possibly the malignancy you perceive in the other is a projection of the negative areas in your own life that are difficult to admit.

The third lens through which to view the problem is the lens of group dynamics. At times, there can be free-floating anxiety infecting a group. The group's unconscious way to handle this is to find someone to blame for what is wrong or uncomfortable within the group. In family systems, this person would be described as the 'identified patient.' This dynamic of scapegoating is a common group defense, which takes its name from an Old Testament concept. When members of a group want to avoid dealing with their own problems, they find someone in the group to scapegoat. The group blames that person for all that is wrong and then attempts to drive that person out of the group. The unspoken hope is that in expelling the 'problem person' the problems in the group will be healed. Of course, that doesn't happen and the group is either forced to find another scapegoat or face their individual problems. Don Jackson, a renowned psychiatrist, brought great insight to this dynamic when he discovered that when you cure a schizophrenic child in some families another child would become schizophrenic. It is a startling revelation of how sometimes the 'difficult person' may in actuality be a 'sacrificial offering' to expiate for the sins of the group. Some groups need a scapegoat, or a difficult person, to allay the free-floating anxiety within the group.

Remember that it is not only individuals who can be scapegoated. Groups, cultures, ethnic groups, and minorities in general are often the victims of this insidious group defense.

A Negative Example

A rather notorious 'dysfunctional' parish had been the cross of a number of pastors. These pastors had a history of being very pastoral and effective in their previous parishes. Within the first six months of the appointment of each new pastor, the bishop would receive a contingent of irate parishioners who demanded the removal of the pastor. The litany of complaints always followed a similar pattern: The priest was a problem and was causing irreparable harm to the parish. Those in the neighboring parishes were convinced that it was not the pastor who was the problem—it was the parishioners in this rural parish who had long-standing feuds that had festered for generations, and they were unwilling to confront the 'elephant in the room.' The sad commentary on this situation was that the bishop was fearful of conflict and would constantly succumb to the demands of the people and remove the pastor. Needless to say, he lost the respect of the priests.

A Positive Example

A leadership group sought assistance in dealing with difficult people. We asked them to identify the 'difficult people' with whom they were dealing. At the conclusion of the exercise they arrived at three insights. First, some of the people had also been identified as difficult by previous leaders and probably were difficult people to deal with.

Second, some of the people had not been perceived as difficult by the previous leaders, and that might possibly be an indication of relational problems between the present leadership and those perceived as problem. That insight challenged the leadership to explore areas where they might have to change, where, in fact, they might be the problem.

Third, while there were many different reasons that were ascribed to why the people were difficult, they discovered a common characteristic in a number of them. They were psychologically underdeveloped. That insight challenged the leaders to determine how they could use their leadership role to initiate responses to rectify that. They organized continuing educational programs that offered the members knowledge that helped them in their journey toward fuller maturation. They also referred individuals to existing programs that might benefit them.

Stop and Think

Identify someone whom you have labeled a 'difficult person.' Can you think of that person in terms of the principle of multiple causality? Can you identify a number of possible reasons for his or her problem behavior? Does that provide you with any new insights as a leader in terms of working with that person?

Reflecting on that same individual, or another person with whom you have had problems, look at the individual through the principle of multiple lenses. Which of the three possibilities listed might be operative?

There are probably individuals who find you difficult. Can you identify the areas where you may have to change to become less difficult to others?

Principle 21: *Be a vision maker*

◇◇

'Where there is no vision, the people perish' (Prv 29:18). This is wise counsel for anyone in leadership. In an interview titled 'The Pastor as Vision Maker,' Father Bill Bausch, who is well known for his exemplary writings on parish leadership, credited much of his success to his role as a vision maker. The Church that emerged in the documents of the Second Vatican Counsel had excited him. He then shared this vision and excitement with the members of his parish. Father Bausch never imposed his vision, but through systematic adult catechesis he shared the vision of the Church articulated by the participants in this historic council. His excitement was contagious. The members of the parish 'caught' this vision, added their own unique insights to it, and it became a shared vision.

Leaders with a vision are life-filled. Their sense of vitality flames a contagion that animates and excites those who share it. This is particularly needed in our times when hopelessness is often an endemic aspect of our society. Many individuals have jettisoned their dreams and hopes and settled for survival. Their language betrays their basic stance toward life. Conversations are filled with stating their ability to last, to survive, to get by, certainly not declarations of vision and enthusiasm. The World Health Organization defines health as the ability to do more than survive, but rather to grow and to prosper. When people are willing to settle for a survival mentality, they have begun the inevitable process of dying. It is the responsibility of the leader to reanimate the individuals or group with a hope for what can be, for a vision. Therefore, it is important that the leader has a vision about which he or she is filled with enthusiasm.

A pessimistic attitude of survival and dying is contrary to our call as Christians. The Gospel of John boldly declares that we are called to be people of light and life, not survival. In the tenth chapter of John, we hear Jesus proclaim 'I have come that you may have life and have it to the full' (Jn 10:10). There are many passages in the Gospel that proclaim that the choice for any Christian must be a choice for life and not survival. Again, we find in John's Gospel: 'The water I shall give them will become within them a fountain of water leaping up unto eternal life' (Jn 4:14). Gospel people are called to life, never to mere survival. John is a leader who espouses a life-filled and life-giving vision. The Old Testament also counsels, 'Choose life.' (Dt.. 30:19).

Individuals who succumb to a survival syndrome are often depressed individuals devoid of any sense of hope. As indicated in a previous chapter, the leaders will only be credible in challenging others beyond this depressive attitude to the degree that they themselves are perceived as persons who are life-filled. We have encountered a large number of Church leaders who epitomize what it means to be 'burned out.' They have no life and they do not energize others. Many have lost the vision that initially propelled them into ministry. Unless they can recapture that vision, their leadership will be counterproductive and they will repel rather than attract people to follow them.

A Negative Example

A large urban parish was known for the number of activities it sponsored.

Even a casual perusal of the parish bulletin was exhausting. The problem was that the frenetic activity did not result in a movement toward accomplishing the mission for which this parish and all parishes exist—to evangelize. The leaders were more interested in extolling their varied activities than in striving toward achieving mission. The various groups often worked in competition with each other to see who could raise the most money or attract the most publicity. What they lacked, pure and simple, was an integrated vision. Activity, when it is not directed, leads to exhaustion and burnout, not to mission.

A Positive Example

One of the most effective leaders we have ever encountered is a priest who exudes life. Even as he ages, he maintains an interest in every one and every thing around him. He has a thirst for acquiring new knowledge and exposes himself to fields of discipline that he never had a chance to pursue in his younger years. His interests are broad, extending to the arts, sports, history, politics, and science. His vitality is like a magnet attracting people to him. He truly exudes a zest for life because from the very beginning of his ministry, he focused on trying to ascertain where and how God was calling him. His vision for himself was to continue to grow in many ways each day. He was a vibrant leader, who attracted others to him and to his vision.

Stop and Think

How clearly can you articulate your vision as a leader? Does that vision continue to change as circumstances change, or has it become a static vision?

Are you aware of times in your own life when you have followed leaders because of the exciting vision that they espoused?

Are you willing to ask a few friends or co-ministers if they would be able to articulate the vision that drives you?

The Leader as Change Agent

◇◇◇

Jesus was a leader who fostered change. He was sent to bring a new vision, 'a new heaven.' Jesus was never the agent of maintaining the status quo. He preached whatever was of God. Sometimes that meant building on what already existed under the Old Covenant, but just as often it meant helping the people see what was new, what was of God, what was life-giving. Perhaps this is most evident when we encounter Jesus in the temple, driving out the money changers.

> They came to Jerusalem, and on entering the Temple area he began to drive out those selling and buying there. He overturned the tables of the money changers and the seats of those who were selling doves. He did not permit anyone to carry anything through the temple area. Then he taught them saying, 'Is it not written: 'My house shall be

called a house of prayer for all peoples'? But you
have made it a den of thieves.'

—Mark 11:15–17

The role of the moneychanger and the buying and selling of
goods in the Temple were time-honored practices in the Jewish
community of the first century. But simply because something has
perdured does not mean it is of God.

Christian leaders, like Jesus, are called to be change agents, a
role that may not be very attractive. It is, after all, what got Jesus
crucified. Church leaders as change agents are not about changing things for the sake of change. They advocate change that will
foster the furthering of the Kingdom of God.

Effective leaders know that when a group's emotions and
interpersonal dynamics get in the way of its task, the leader must
refocus the group on the process before proceeding. It is impossible to achieve the purpose, the mission, the Kingdom, when a
variety of circumstances are preventing this. Effective group leaders learn to focus on maintaining a healthy and rewarding process,
rather than plodding along toward the goal or mission without
due regard to whatever emotional and relational distress may be
resulting from the group's work.

The principles in this final chapter focus on a variety of disciplines needed for change leadership with individuals and within
groups:

- Learning the difficult task of staying with the pain when the
  pain motivates the individual or group toward growth
- Developing additional skills beyond the verbal skills of teaching and preaching
- Acquiring a basic attitude of seeing those you work with as
  allies rather than adversaries
- Embracing resistance as a potential for growth

- Asking the 'why' behind the 'what' question
- Realizing that parallel process is a dynamic often at work in personal and communal relationships
- Valuing the gifts that each culture brings to the mission
- Never labeling
- Becoming aware of the intense dynamics that occur in all relationships
- Being compassionate and competent

Principle 22: *Stay with the pain*

An effective pastoral leader advised us to 'stay with the pain' when working with others. What sounds so simple, in reality, is very difficult. Many Church leaders resist allowing others to be in pain. We found ourselves resisting. 'Good' Christians, after all, believe that they bear a responsibility, if not a gospel imperative, to remove pain. However, emotional or psychological pain can be a major motivator for change, just like physical pain can motivate an injured or ill person to take whatever actions are needed to recover. Removing pain often eliminates the motivation.

In supervising leaders, we have sometimes had to endure anger as we discouraged them from attempting to remove the pain of those with whom they worked. We were perceived as cruel and heartless for suggesting such a course of action. We are not advocating a hostile response, but rather, one that is motivated by concern, care, and compassion. To simply remove another's pain is often a disrespectful thing to do and eliminates the only solid motivation for improving the situation that yielded the pain in the first place.

Pain comes in many varieties. There is physical, psychological, and emotional pain. Clark Moustakis, the author of a classic work on loneliness, described the excruciating pain of loneliness. He also encouraged his readers to embrace loneliness and the pain that frequently accompanies it. It is in the very act of embracing loneliness that one is forced to enter into the depths of one's being and to engage in the difficult but productive work of self-exploration. It can be in loneliness that one comes to experience the God who is at the center of all being.

Generally, our culture has such an aversion to pain, suffering, and loneliness that the almost immediate, unconscious reaction is to escape into activity. One has only to watch an evening's worth of television commercials and note how many products claim to reduce or eliminate pain or discomfort. But in immediately acting to reduce our pain, especially psychological pain, we are easily robbed of the insight that can be gained through confronting it.

There are many reasons why 'good' Christians attempt to remove pain. Frequently, of course, we are motivated by genuine compassion and a desire to help. At other times, we attempt to remove another's pain because the pain in the other makes us uncomfortable and forces us to confront our own humanness, mortality, and vulnerability. So, attempting to take the pain away from others is often an unconscious attempt to bring relief to oneself. At still other times, the desire to eliminate another's pain is really an unconscious way of increasing one's own sense of potency: 'Look at how powerful I am. I can take away pain.' The lower the self-esteem, the more likely this is to be a key motivator.

When people are in pain, they generally experience increased stress. Stress, like pain, should not be removed too swiftly. Hans Selye, the Canadian researcher and world-renowned expert on stress, put this succinctly: 'The absence of stress is death!' Our pastoral goal is to help people choose life. Sometimes this requires that leaders practice the difficult discipline of allowing others to have their pain.

Of course, the challenge for the pastoral leader is to find the balance—providing a compassionate response while allowing the person to maintain enough pain to motivate her or him to change. Most find it difficult to achieve this balance and may err on the side of activity, doing what one can to remove the pain. Often, supervision or consultation will be extremely helpful in making this discernment.

A Negative Example

A community of women religious engaged the services of a facilitator to help resolve some lingering conflict among the members. At various times during the ensuing meetings, one sister continually sat on the periphery of the group, with arms and legs wrapped tightly around herself. Her eyes were often filled with tears, and it was evident that the discussions were causing her extreme pain. Any attempts on the part of the facilitator to engage her in the dialog were met with her emotional withdrawal. The other sisters tried to engage the withdrawing member, and her repressed tears would pour forth abundantly. Rather than explore what was happening, the facilitator began to protect the fearful sister and generated a myriad of excuses for allowing her to remain uninvolved. Needless to say, there was no growth in either that particular sister or within the community.

A Positive Example

Mary Jones was a sixty-year-old married woman and spiritual director at a retreat center. Her directee was a talented, newly ordained priest who was struggling with his first assignment. He had been ordained less than a year. His pastor was a domineering person who had a propensity to belittle others when he felt threatened or insecure. The pastor would criticize the young priest's homilies in the presence of parishioners. The young priest also reported that he heard the pastor belittling him and criticizing him to other priests at the clergy conference. He was searching to find God's will and reported to Mary that he had serious thoughts of leaving the priesthood.

At times, this young priest looked so pathetic and forlorn when he was recounting his struggles that Mary's maternal instincts would kick in and she had a desire to hug and comfort him. Instead, she would remain quiet and then ask difficult questions that would sometimes exacerbate his pain. Finally, she helped him to realize that if he wanted to reduce the pain, he had to take some initiative. She asked him what he thought God was asking of him. The young priest decided to see his bishop and explain the situation. The bishop, a very pastoral, compassionate man, reassigned him, and the young priest blossomed in his new parish.

Stop and Think

Visualize someone in pain with whom you are working. Can you identify your honest reaction to that pain? Are you aware of any tendencies to take the pain away?

Have you ever had a helper or leader who has attempted to remove your pain? What was your reaction—to resist their attempts or to passively allow the other to attempt to remove the pain? Was the situation a growth-producing one?

The next time you are working with someone who is psychologically or emotionally hurting, attempt to get in touch with your own emotions and tendencies. What

are some of the reasons why you would choose to try to
eliminate their pain?

Principle 23: *Avoid preaching and teaching*

◇◇

Previous generations of religious leaders were trained to be
effective teachers or preachers. Both are valuable leadership
skills. However, when these skills are used exclusively in all pastoral situations, they are often counterproductive. It has been our
experience that the least effective leaders are those who revert to
teaching and preaching in situations that instead call for listening
and dialogue. When leaders embrace an attitude and stance of
teachers or preachers, they often suspend their listening skills.

Researcher George Gallup discovered that an extremely small
percentage of people (less than 4 percent) obtain truth from listening to religious leaders. Roughly 42 percent of those interviewed
discovered truth from reflection on their experiences. The conclusion is obvious: Effective leaders are much more adept at listening to people and helping them discover the truth, strength, and
grace within themselves than in communicating 'truth.' Those
who assume a stance of teacher or preacher are more self-focused
than other-focused.

We have been privileged to offer group leadership training
workshops. Some individuals seem to have an almost innate ability

to lead groups, and the training simply provides them with additional tools to be more effective. Some individuals do not have the natural talent, but through disciplined application of theory, they can develop into effective group leaders. Those whom we found most difficult to train were those individuals whose primary training was teaching and preaching. Leadership of groups frequently produces anxiety. A frequent response to anxiety is to revert to what one knows best. In the case of these individuals, they revert to their teaching and preaching skills when the situation calls for something else.

In order to understand your behavior or that of another, you must think *needs*. Consciously or unconsciously, one's behavior is in response to a need that is present. It is a good rule of thumb that when an individual leader constantly reverts to a teaching or preaching modality, there is a strong possibility that the person is feeling a threat to his or her self-esteem.

A Negative Example

While facilitating a pastoral group, we were impressed by the intensity with which the group members listened to and attended to whomever was speaking. Then we became aware of a shift in attitude and the listening stance was no longer present. We discovered that every time a certain person spoke, he gave a little 'ferverino' to the assembled group. He preached to them, even though he was one of the youngest members of the group. His preaching was perceived by the others as a sign of disrespect, and it was met with boredom and inattention. When he finished preaching and another member of the group spoke, the group immediately returned to attentive listening. We commented on this phenomenon to the group, but are not sure that the 'preacher' was willing or capable of hearing the feedback or of changing his behavior.

A Positive Example

One effective group leader was a woman recognized by her peers as an outstanding teacher. She had achieved tenure as a professor of sociology at the university where she was employed. She had also volunteered to lead support groups for homeless women two evenings a week. The purpose of the group was to allow the women to share their emotions, especially their fears and shame of living on the street. As a professor she taught urban issues, but she never lectured the women. She believed that they had the ability to assist one another. Her role, as she saw it, was to create a safe environment where these vulnerable women were able to discuss issues that overwhelmed them. She never felt the need to revert to being a teacher to the group, realizing they would learn far more from one another and find greater strength in their sharing.

Stop and Think

Have you been part of a group where the leader began preaching or teaching when the group needed dialogue? What impact did it have on you? What was your response or reaction to that person? What was the group's response?

Are you aware of the times when you revert to being a teacher or preacher? Can you identify whether the cause is anxiety? If so, are you aware of what causes such anxiety in you?

How do you deal with individuals who believe their purpose in life is to preach to or teach you?

Principle 24: *Focus on others as allies, rather than adversaries*

◇◇

Perception plays a major role in leadership. You can choose to focus on those you lead as allies or as adversaries. This simple principle can change one's whole approach to leadership. Even when the leader's words are positive and affirming, the other will intuit the basic adversarial attitude of the leader if it is present. If you perceive the other as an adversary, that person can actually become an adversary. The meta-communication (the communication of feelings more than the words) is transmitted. This is true both when leading individuals as well as groups. An adversarial relationship bodes poorly for developing constructive leadership alliances.

There is a beautiful passage in the book *Tuesdays with Morrie* when the author, Mitch Albom, describes a touching interchange between himself and Morrie. Mitch asks if there is any wisdom that Morrie can share to predict if a marriage will be successful. Morrie's initial response is, 'Things are not that simple, Mitch.' However, after some further thought he offers four 'rules.' These rules are not only criteria for predicting a successful marriage, but also insightful rules for any leader attempting to create a positive alliance. The rules are simple: communicate mutual respect; remain open to compromise; be completely honest; and begin from an acknowledgement of shared values. We offer these four criteria for the personal reflection of leaders. Picture those for whom you have some leadership responsibility.

• Are others able to sense your respect for them?

- Do you leave room for compromise, or are your ideas communicated in a way that does not allow for dialogue or compromise?
- How honest are you with others, even when the reaction to your honesty may be hostility?
- Have you taken the time to assure that a common set of shared values exists between you?

Cardinal Kaspar, president of the Pontifical Council for Promoting Christian Unity, said that since the Second Vatican Council, 'dialogue has become a fundamental expression and feature of Catholicism.' He indicated that when attempting to build Christian unity, it is important to search for areas of agreement and then to 'let the disagreements surface.' He believes that this dialog must begin from a perspective of dignity, integrity, and freedom of the other. In assuming this attitude, one is starting from a position of alliance and not an adversarial one.

A Negative Example

While conducting a workshop for pastoral councils, a participant presented a question that we had heard many times before: 'Can you make any suggestions about what we can do with our pastor?' The question communicated the basic attitude of the questioner. The pastor was perceived as a 'problem,' an adversary. We were certain that the pastor, unless he was completely oblivious, must have been aware of how he was perceived by this parishioner. Our response to the question seemed to initially surprise the questioner. We simply asked, 'What are the gifts of the pastor?' After a moment's hesitation, he began enumerating some of the pastor's positive qualities. He then confessed that he had only been looking at the pastor's inadequacies and not his positive attributes. As a result, both the questioner and the pastor were in a constant adversarial position. It is our hope that as a result of the insight the parishioner gained, his attitude toward the pastor changed. Hopefully, he then viewed him as an ally and not an adversary in their future interactions.

A Positive Example

We were invited to facilitate a potentially contentious national meeting. The participants were primarily priests and women who worked together in pastoral ministry. The organizers informed us that one issue was dividing the group and would probably cause conflict. Not surprisingly, the issue of conflict dealt with the liturgy, often the lightning rod for pent-up hostility among Catholic leaders. The identified problem was that most of the priests were planning to vest and concelebrate at Mass during the gathering. This offended a number of the women.

Prior to the liturgy we invited the group to break into smaller groups, each composed of both priests and women. We then asked each woman to tell the priests what it is like for her, as a woman, to be working in the church. We challenged the priests to listen attentively and, hopefully non-defensively, to the women. We then did the same with the priests, requesting that each priest share what it is like for him to be a priest ministering in today's church. The women were likewise challenged to listen with a spirit of openness to the priests. For almost one hour each group engaged in intense dialogue. When their discussions were completed, we asked what they had learned. Not surprisingly, they discovered that they had much in common and experienced very similar feelings. During the course of listening to one another, it was evident that their attitude had changed from an adversarial one to a more collaborative one.

Stop and Think

Are you aware of a time when you sensed antipathy in another even though the words did not convey this? What effect did it have on you?

Picture the person with whom you have the most difficulty working with collaboratively. What is your basic stance toward this person? Is it adversarial or positive? Are you willing to consider changing this stance if it is interfering with your ability to be a more effective leader?

Leading any group, especially angry, hostile ones, often produces anxiety. Anxiety often precludes an ability to see the positive aspects of the other. The next time you are leading a group, ask yourself, 'Do I see these individuals as allies or adversaries?'

Principle 25: *Recognize resistance as a normal dynamic*

◇◇

Leaders are often described as change agents. Being an agent of change is one of the more difficult aspects of leadership.

Most individuals and organizations resist change. There is a tendency toward homeostasis, to maintain what is, and to resist anything that challenges the familiar. This is often true even when the familiar is not comfortable or is perhaps even painfully dysfunctional.

Change of any nature will usually be met with resistance. There are a number of very logical, though unconscious, reasons for this. First, deviation from what is known and secure produces anxiety. The normal response to anxiety, as mentioned before, is to incorporate a defense. Ironically, even when the change has a positive potential outcome, you can expect that there will be a great deal of energy expended to avoid the change. This dynamic happens with individuals and with groups. A leader initiating change within an organization must expect to meet resistance and less-than-enthusiastic responses. This is true of any organization, be that an office staff, a family, religious community, ministry group, pastoral staff, faculty, or any other group committed to a common purpose. The human person has an amazing ability to change and adapt, but rarely does so instantaneously or as a result of the leader's rhetoric. This is a normal dynamic that must run its course. Change only takes place after anxiety diminishes. Only then can you expect an openness and willingness to try something new. Even then, don't expect that there will be an initial embracing of the change. The leader's role is to facilitate this movement by creating a climate of openness that decreases the intensity of the anxiety.

There is at least one other reason why resistance is the normal reaction to change. Any change in the present, resurrects the 'unfinished business' from previous losses. When individuals or groups experience loss, grieving will follow. Grieving is a very necessary but painful process. The pain produced by loss is rarely 'worked through' to completion. Most people realize, at some level, that if they were ever to adequately enter into the grieving process of major losses in their lives, it might lead to depression. The human mind and spirit in healthy people triggers a merciful response that distances itself from the pain of grieving when there is a possibility to do so. However, since the grieving is not completed, it is resurrected with any loss, no matter how seemingly insignificant, in the present. This is, therefore, one of the reasons for the resistance to change and a reason why leaders often see a disproportionate reaction to seemingly minor and insignificant losses. Dealing with change means dealing with the painful unfinished business.

Resistance to change may not only be a normal response, but at times, it is a healthy response. Brother James Zullo, in an article in *Human Development*, commented on the positive aspects of resistance. In discussing alcoholism, he indicated that resistance is energy. He claims that the energy that is expended in resisting change can be harnessed and used to foster growth. It should be of greater concern, he says, when resistance is replaced by apathy or passivity. The prognosis for growth is negligible when there is passivity rather than resistance. The possibility for growth is much greater when the energy of resistance is present.

When dealing with change, leaders should remember that change and loss are not headaches, they are heartaches. Simply trying to intellectually convince those faced with change of its benefits will probably be met with skepticism and possible rejection. The role of the leader is to listen to the heart of the other. Allow them to begin to articulate their reasons for resistance. The chance for accepting change is enhanced when individuals believe that they have been listened to and understood.

A Negative Example

A newly appointed department chairperson held a meeting and announced numerous policy and procedural changes for the whole department. The existing policies were not perfect, but they were effective and they worked. The proposed changes were not, in and of themselves, bad, and in some instances the changes offered more effective and improved methods. However, the chair met with marked resistance from everyone in the department. There was a great deal of complaining, non-cooperation, and lack of support. In a short time the general morale of the department sunk to an all-time low as energy got short-circuited by resistance to the chair. Eventually, the effectiveness of the department's mission and purpose suffered.

A Positive Example

A pastor who had been dearly loved and respected by his previous parish was assigned to another parish, replacing another dearly loved pastor. The new pastor possessed a special gift for creating sacred space. Within a month of his arrival at the parish, he began to make significant changes in the sanctuary, including the removal of a statue that had graced the sanctuary for decades. Objectively and aesthetically, the worship space was transformed into a much more spiritual and reflective atmosphere. When a group of parishioners showed up at the rectory door, he presumed they were there to affirm him for what he had done. This was not the case. They were there to vent their hostility for the changes he had made in 'their' church. His initial reaction was hurt and defensiveness. However, he soon realized that his actions had triggered some intense and hostile responses. He invited the parishioners into the living room, offered them coffee, and asked them to explain to him why they were so upset. What emerged were a myriad of feelings. Their families had built the church and purchased the statue that was removed. In addition, he soon realized that they had not been given the opportunity to grieve the loss of the previous pastor. He listened patiently to them and asked them to help him organize a town meeting so he could listen to the people. The resistance slowly diminished and was replaced with a spirit of collaboration between the parishioners and the new pastor.

Stop and Think

Think of a time when you were being invited or forced to change. What was your reaction? How did you express your resistance? Was anything done that helped you to be open to consider the change?

What have been your most positive and negative experiences of change? What can you learn from both?

What helped you to move beyond your initial resistance to change? What does this say to you as a leader?

Principle 26: *Explore the why behind the what*

◇◇◇

A popular magazine contained a striking ad in large white letters emboldened on a vivid red background that read 'Never stop asking WHY!' Introductory psychology courses often discourage asking the question, 'Why?' The rationale for such advice makes eminent sense. On the one hand, the persons being helped often do not know why they are doing what they are doing. Motivation for behavior is often unconscious. Such questions can cause frustration and commensurate feelings of guilt when the individuals are unable to come up with any cogent reasons for their behavior.

On the other hand, when there is a high degree of anxiety or conflict in an individual or group, asking why may be of great help. When conflict emerges, people are in an aroused emotional state. In such a state there are generally three faculties that 'shut down.' People don't think clearly, they don't speak rationally, and they don't act compassionately. They simply react to whatever threat is stirred by the conflict. When the entire group is engaged in conflict, there is often a contagion of irrational thinking and acting. The perceived threat to the self is often compensated for by a compulsive need to talk. Generally, the talking is accompanied by a lack of listening. If everyone in the group feels the same, that is, that no one is listening to them, the conflict escalates. One of the most useful things that leaders can do at this juncture is to slow people down. A leader might pick up on something just shared and ask, 'Why do you believe or feel that?' In all likelihood, the very act of asking the question breaks the contagion. If done in a caring way, it can also communicate a sincere interest in knowing what others think and feel. Someone is demonstrating an interest in *them.*

Asking why is not only appropriate and recommended in group situations; it can also be effective one-on-one. Its effectiveness will depend on the perception of why and how the question is being asked. If the other perceives the question as a threat or judgment, a defensive response may follow. However, asking why can also be perceived as a desire to understand the other and an invitation to dialogue and insights.

Sometimes asking why can be an invitation to self-reflection. It invites individuals to reflect more deeply on what they are saying and forces them to articulate the significance of what they share.

An organizational development colleague of ours claims that in applying organizational development theory, the primary approach is to ask questions rather than to offer solutions or apply techniques or theories.

Finally, asking why clearly demonstrates a keen interest in the other. We ran across an anonymous saying that eminently captures the wisdom of asking people to explain their reasons for their beliefs or behaviors: 'The way to impress people is not by telling them how wonderful you are. If you want to impress people, you need to listen to how wonderful they are.'

A Negative Example

A colleague shared a poignant story about the value of asking why, and the disastrous effects of not posing this probing question. While serving as a Peace Corps volunteer in a rural mountain area in South America, he was invited to work with a community to help find a solution to a perplexing problem. They needed a bridge built to span a vast gorge. He immediately began to plan for the building of the bridge, which seemed like a relatively easy task. At that point, an elderly man spoke. He offered some counsel: 'Senor, before you go about planning how to build the bridge, why don't you first ask why it hasn't yet been built?' The question startled our colleague. Only then did he ask the why. When he did so, he learned that if the bridge were built, it would take the members of this community directly through an area occupied by a group who had been their lifelong enemies. Failure to ask why would have led to the building of an extraneous bridge that would never be used by the people.

A Positive Example

After we conducted a program in a parish, one of the parishioners asked to talk with us. The night before we had asked the program participants to reflect on and share when they had experienced ministry, when they had felt ministered to. The woman had not shared her experience during the session but was very anxious to share it with us now. She mentioned a time when she went to confession and confessed a particular sin that had been bothering her for a long time. After confessing the sin, she informed the priest that there had been some extenuating circumstances that led up to the act. She began crying as she said, 'He didn't talk about the sin, he just kept asking me questions about the extenuating circumstances.' She repeated this a number of times as the tears continued to flow. She described what a healing experience this had been for her. The priest had not condemned her, but rather he showed a concern for her and her perceptions of the incident. She left the confessional feeling understood, healed, and cared for.

Stop and Think

Have you ever been asked to explain the reason why you feel so strongly about a particular situation? What was your reaction to the request? Did you find it helpful? If so, why?

Recall someone who has been helpful to you in a one-on-one situation. What did that person do or say to create a healing climate for you?

Recall the last time you were in a conflictual situation within a group. Can you get in touch with what was happening within you? Were you able to listen and respond in a coherent manner? What could the leader have done to create a climate that would be conducive to both individual and group growth?

Principle 27: *Recognize parallel process*

◇◇

Effective leaders are conscious of a dynamic called 'parallel process.' Parallel process is a phenomenon whereby individuals who are having difficulty with some aspect of their personal or professional life attempt to discover effective ways for resolving the difficulty by unconsciously projecting the dilemma onto another, especially someone in a leadership position. This is achieved by behaving toward the leader in the same manner that the people they are having difficulty with act toward them. Without being fully aware of it, they hope that the leader's response will provide them with more positive and productive ways of dealing with these difficult situations in the future.

It was a supervisor who first made us aware of this dynamic. Some time later, a student we were supervising presented an interesting case. She had just conducted a counseling group that she left feeling extremely vulnerable and helpless. The student was unable to identify any apparent reasons for her feelings. During the supervision session with us, it became apparent that helplessness and vulnerability accurately described what many members of the counseling group were feeling as they tried to cope with

their work and personal lives. Without any apparent justifica-
tion, the group also began to become angry toward the leader.
Although the group members did not directly address these issues
of vulnerability, helplessness, and anger in the group sessions, the
group was able to project these feelings onto the group leader.

Our student had no inclination of what was occurring or any
insight about how to deal with it. Without realizing what she was
doing, she presented her group experience in supervision in such
a convoluted way that we found ourselves experiencing a sense
of powerlessness. In addition, because of our inability to provide
her with any useful feedback, she became increasingly hostile
toward us. This was classic parallel process at work on more than
one level. Our student was unconsciously projecting her emotions
onto us in an attempt to learn how to deal more effectively with
them. Because of what we had learned from our supervisor, we
were able to help her understand the dynamic that was occurring
at both levels. The group had projected their feelings onto her.
Because she felt frustrated, she, in turn, placed us in a situation
where we experienced the same feelings. In pointing this out to
her, she was able to address her own emotions and in turn help
the group understand what was happening. She led them in creating a climate in which they were able to openly discuss what they
were feeling and to explore ways for dealing with those feelings in
a more productive manner.

The more leaders become aware of the existence of parallel
process, the more effective they will be in helping others. The
learning begins with a principle we suggested earlier, trusting your
gut. This is especially important when the emotions being experienced seem to have no relevance to the situation at hand. Getting
in touch with this phenomenon on one's own is usually difficult.
Here, again, is a situation in which a supervisor or consultant can
be of great benefit, as we have repeatedly suggested.

A Negative Example

While working in a center for battered women I met on a regular basis with one of the residents, Carla. Our previous sessions had gone well, and I believed we were developing a rapport and a helping relationship where I could be of greater service to her. Five minutes into the session she began to become extremely hostile toward me. I knew I had done nothing to provoke the verbal, abusive tirade that was directed toward me. I feared that she was about to both verbally and physically attack me. I remember feeling extremely fearful and called for some backup from other staff members. I reacted solely on my feelings rather than following the useful paradigm to feel-think-talk-act. Later, in reflecting on the incident, I became aware of what had occurred. Carla had inserted me into a situation of parallel process. I was feeling everything she had been experiencing, especially fear, but because of my inability to comprehend what was occurring, I missed the opportunity to assist her with her fears.

A Positive Example

A director of priest personnel in a diocese recounted this experience. At the height of media coverage about the clergy abuse scandals in the United States, he was designated by his bishop to meet with priests in deanery gatherings. Initially, the director returned from each of the meetings and reported to his peers on the curial staff that he felt alienated after each of the meetings. In addition, he had a sense that the group was angry with him and perceived him as a bad and evil person. When talking this over with one of his personnel consultants, the director began to become aware of the dynamic of parallel process as it was being acted out in these meetings. Once he was able to distance himself from his subjective reaction and look objectively at what his emotions were telling him about how the priests felt, he was able to approach the meetings in a much more productive way. When he was in touch with his feelings, he immediately made the connection to what they were feeling.

Realizing that they were feeling alienated, he posed a question to them: 'What is it like to be a priest today: are any of you experiencing a sense of feeling alienated or reviled?' The simple question, asked without explaining the concept of parallel process, created an inviting environment for the priests to talk about what they were experiencing.

Stop and Think

Are you aware of any times when you felt overwhelmed by some emotion after working with an individual or group? Can you recall who composed the group, what issues the members were facing, and how your feelings may have been a reflection or projection of their emotions? How might you respond to such a group in the future?

Can you identify times when you were having difficulty in a relationship with an individual or a group? Are you aware now of how you may have unconsciously involved another in parallel process to help find a solution to the problem?

How would you explain the dynamic of parallel process to someone else?

Principle 28: *Think culture*

◇◇

Multiculturalism is both a gift to the Church and a profound challenge for pastoral leaders. For instance, it is not uncommon in the United States for a pastoral leader to be of a different culture than the persons being served. Likewise, it is becoming increasingly more common today for Church groups to be composed of many different cultures. We recently ministered in a diocese where almost every parish was trilingual. There is at least one archdiocese in the United States where the liturgy is celebrated in over fifty languages every weekend. This is a major change from the Church of the not-too-distant-past in which most parishes were composed of one, or at the most two, distinctive cultures. As a child I grew up in a Euro-centered Church, populated mostly by Irish Catholics, some of German decent, and a sprinkling of Italians. At the time, that was the extent of multiculturalism.

In group leadership training we learned, both from the theory presented and from our personal experience as group leaders, that the more homogenous a group is, the quicker it is to coalesce and achieve minor tasks. By contrast, the more heterogeneous and diverse a group is, the longer it takes to coalesce, but the greater its capacity to resolve more complex issues. Therefore, multicultural groups, with good leadership, have a greater potential for achieving the difficult task of advancing the Kingdom.

During our group leadership training, we were also introduced to the concept of group stages. During the early life of groups, the stages of in–out and up–down are both prominent. During the in–out stage, there are some members of the group who feel as though they belong, while others feel excluded or alienated. During the up–down stages, the group sorts itself out along a continuum of the most valued to the least valued members. In multicultural groups, it is often those representing a minority culture who feel both alienated and devalued. Such a scenario is an almost sure-fire predictor for conflict.

Any one who has been a leader in a multicultural setting realizes that each culture holds certain values and norms that are implicitly neither positive nor negative, but constitutive of that group's cultural identity. These values and norms affect every aspect of their lives. Only leaders who take the time to learn the specific values and norms of the various cultures will be effective pastoral leaders. Following are two examples of such values and norms.

> Maria, a Mexican American pastoral leader, recounted the story of a friend asking her mother who her oldest child was. Without a pause her mother responded 'Juan.' Maria spontaneously responded, 'No, it's Tina!' Her mother responded, 'But she's a girl.' Maria reported that this was an example of how women in her culture were perceived. They were invisible.

A Hispanic/Latino friend decries the fact that the deprived Anglos seem only able to do one thing at a time. He, on the other hand—because of his cultural background—is able to do many things at once and engage in a number of conversations at the same time. However, he claims that such behavior is often perceived as rude by those who can only carry on one conversation at a time.

While conducting a workshop for a group from an Asian culture, one of our team members commented that I seemed rather quiet and reticent. I informed him that I knew very little about the culture of the group with whom we were working. He suggested that I understood human nature and suggested I proceed from that knowledge and add the culture as an overlay to the universal human experiences. I found his advice to be extremely helpful. As human beings, we experience the same emotions, drives, and needs. Once we acknowledge this, we can sensitively add cultural dimensions to our interactions and relationships.

There are a number of commonly held misconceptions that can impede pastoral effectiveness. Among these are: 1) People who speak a common language share a common culture. 2) All people from a culture share the same beliefs, attitudes, and behaviors. 3) Culture is restricted to ethnicity.

Language and culture are two separate variants. Again, it was our Hispanic/Latino friend who shared the experience of writing an article comparing Cubans and Puerto Ricans, emphasizing their differences, and probably managing to alienate both groups in the process. The two groups may share a common language, but much about each of these two cultures is quite distinct from the other.

Another misconception often held by inexperienced leaders in multicultural settings is to stereotype members because of their ethnic culture. It's part of the 'that's the way *they* are' syndrome. We were recently working with a group where we heard those very words uttered. Not only was the stereotype offensive, it was inaccurate. Sometimes stereotyping can be an anxiety-reducing mechanism utilized by those who feel unprepared to work with certain cultures. Feeling different can initiate the stereotypical response. Some behavior that is erroneously labeled as cultural is really idiosyncratic. In those cases the observable behavior has little to do with the culture and much to do with the person who is exhibiting the behavior.

A third misconception is that culture is restricted to ethnicity. Effective pastoral leaders are mindful of the cultural differences in each parish. As was earlier alluded to, attempting to apply the same pastoral approaches in each distinct parish will lead to frustration and potential conflict, both for the leaders and members. This is true, for instance, even in parishes that are contiguous. Each parish has its own personal history and will require a pastoral response appropriate for its uniqueness.

Failure to understand and respect cultural values undermines any leadership potential. The more the values of the others are at variance with the values of the leader, the more difficult it is for the leader to understand and value the culture of the other, thus minimizing the leader's potential to lead.

A Negative Example

One of my first assignments as a religious was to an inner-city settlement house. Thirty-plus years after finishing that assignment, I was invited back for a reunion. While the experience was, in general, a positive one, I was painfully aware of how I had brought my white, middle-class, Catholic values into this poor, predominately non-Catholic, African American community. I had the misguided belief that my role as a religious was to 'instill' my values in these people who, in fact, had their own rich cultural tradition, sometimes in conflict with mine. It was during the intervening thirty-plus years that I learned what true evangelization is about. It works both ways, ideally resulting in a blending of what is best in both cultures. At the end of the reunion I sent a letter to each of the attendees to apologize for whatever pain my insensitivity had caused.

A Positive Example

One of the most effective pastoral leaders we have known was a lay missioner from the United States who had been assigned to a Latin American community. Although she had done both her undergraduate and graduate degrees in cross-cultural studies, she arrived at the mission with an attitude as a learner and student. She presumed nothing. She spent her first months there asking the people to teach her about them and their culture. She was a major contrast from many of the previous missionaries who had been there. As a result of her attitude, she developed very strong bonds with the people and was very effective in her missionary labors.

Stop and Think

Think of a time when you were in a situation with someone of a different culture and experienced a sense of alienation. What were your cultural values and beliefs? What were the cultural values and beliefs of the other? How did these values come into conflict? What was done to help bridge the gap and produce meaningful dialogue?

Are you aware of any time a leader helped to effectively bridge the gap between cultures? What was it that he or she did to bridge that gap?

Look around your own neighborhood. Make note of the variety of cultures that are there. Have you ever considered asking some of these neighbors to explain their culture to you?

Principle 29: *Avoid labeling*

◇◇◇

D iagnostic labels are valuable and absolutely essential in therapeutic situations. They provide the therapist with a clear and appropriate direction for a treatment plan. However, outside the therapeutic situation, labeling is usually counterproductive. For instance, labeling someone as a passive-aggressive personality or an angry person usually provokes a defensive reaction. Labeling tends to threaten self-esteem, and when the self-esteem of the labeled person is fragile, the response is often one of anger and hostility. If the leader hopes to help another, labeling undermines those good intentions. We observed someone attending the general chapter of his congregation who had an insight that could have been very valuable for the community to hear. However, he felt so passionately about the issue that he got carried away with the emotion and described the congregation as 'narcissistic and dysfunctional.' Needless to say, his potentially positive intervention was ignored by the group as a result of the negative label that he used to describe them. Most of the rest of the group likely labeled him a malcontent in return, thereby rendering his opinion even less relevant in the group's opinion.

There is an additional negative aspect of labeling. Once leaders label others, they tend to always see those others through the filter of that label. The label becomes a self-fulfilling prophecy. In the mind of the leader, the person tends to become the label, as the following negative example will illustrate.

Labeling limits the potential we can see in another. Sometimes, as leaders, we label ourselves, and that limits our personal and professional horizons. We knew a congregational leader who also presented workshops on personality types. While conducting a gift-discernment process with the leadership team he shared the gifts he perceived in himself. The other members of the team then tried to share other gifts that they saw in him but that he did not identify in himself. After his intense resistance to accepting the gifts described by his peers, one of them said, 'You have some very unique gifts that could be very helpful to this team and to the congregation, but you'll never see them because they don't fit into the personality type by which you have identified yourself.' Truly, he was restricted from seeing his true potential because of the label he had placed on himself.

Labeling is something that appears to be very much in vogue in Church circles today. Individuals can too easily be labeled with such terms as conservative or liberal. In a more subtle way we may label people as a result of their culture, gender, or sexual orientation. In recent years we have been invited to give workshops on the topic 'Men Are from Mars: Women Are from Venus.' The designation is clever but may not always be helpful. Once we label women or men in a certain way, we tend to see all women and men with that label applied to them. As a result, we may not encounter the person but only the stereotype. Labeling may be in vogue because it provides the opportunity to provide simple solutions to complex problems. Labeling can ward off threats to self-esteem when the simple solutions are found to be inadequate.

A Negative Example

The staff of a psychiatric treatment and training center recounted a classic story of labeling. The staff psychiatrist was a well-known and well-respected therapist. However, he also was considered to be a rather vain person. At a staff meeting someone mentioned her lack of success in dealing with a paranoid-schizophrenic, a patient she described as having illusions of grandeur, who believed he was a psychologist. The staff had planned in advance to have this therapist ask the staff psychiatrist to interview the patient behind a one-way mirror. That way, they said, the staff would have the benefit of observing his skill and learning from him. Without the slightest trace of reluctance the psychiatrist agreed to the invitation.

Unknown to this gentleman, the staff had also visited a local hospital and presented a similar story to the hospital's staff psychologist. They informed her that they had a patient at their center who was a paranoid-schizophrenic, one with illusions of grandeur who was convinced he was a psychiatrist. The treatment center's psychiatrist and the hospital psychologist both arrived in the interview room, having labeled the other as paranoid-schizophrenic. For one hour they both tried to break through the pathology and resistance of the other. Meanwhile, the staff was behind the one-way mirror hysterical with laughter. Once we label someone, we tend to perceive them only as we have labeled them.

A Positive Example

We had a dear friend who contracted a degenerative disease of the muscles. He experienced a pretty rapid deterioration that left him unable to do even simple things that he had done for himself in the past. He began to become dependent on his confreres for virtually everything. He was a truly good and holy man. He contacted a spiritual director to help him search for God's will in the midst of his personal tragedy. He explained to us how he spent most of the spiritual direction sessions focusing on his illness. One day he returned from one of the sessions and had a beaming smile on his face. Of course, we had to ask what happened. He explained that about halfway through the session the director cut him off and stated, 'You are more than your illness!' It suddenly struck him that he had defined himself by his illness. He had labeled himself and restricted himself to just one dimension of the unique and special person he was. His spiritual director refused to allow him to be circumscribed by the label of his illness. Our friend acknowledged this intervention as the defining moment in his choice for life and growth rather than just survival.

Stop and Think

Have you ever been labeled by another? What effect did it have on you? How did you respond to the labeler or label?

How does your perception of yourself, the way you have labeled yourself, restrict your ability to acknowledge and utilize the fullness of your gifts and talents?

Have you ever labeled someone or some group by a single characteristic of their total personality, for example, 'an angry person' or 'a dysfunctional group'? Did the label restrict your ability to see the other positive dimensions of those labeled?

Principle 30: *Be competent and compassionate*

What has been your experience with the medical profession? It is probably quite varied, some outstanding interactions and some extremely unpleasant ones. We interviewed people who truly witness their Christian values working in that milieu. One of the interviewees was a doctor, described as outstanding by at least one of his patients. This doctor shared two foundational disciplines that he believes are necessary for being a good leader in the medical field: be competent and be compassionate. Certainly, we want our medical doctors to be competent. It was the concept of compassion that initially surprised us. Upon reflection, it became clear that those doctors who had been most effective in dealing with patients had combined the two attributes of competence and compassion.

When we first considered writing a book on principles for leadership, these dual aspects of competence and compassion continued to surface in our dialogue. To be competent and compassionate are not only the desired prerequisites for good medical practice, they are also the essential elements for any leader, regardless of the context in which leadership is practiced.

During a session on strategic planning, one participant identified a concern that she heard voiced by some of her fellow parishioners. There were recurring questions about the competency of the recently hired staff. Many of these new Church employees were good, generous parishioners who had given freely of their time and energy for many years. However, most of them lacked adequate preparation for the professional role they were now assuming. They may have been very compassionate, but their competency was questionable. The parishioner who raised the concern about the competency of the parish staff commented about the director of religious education, 'I'm entrusting my children to her for their religious education and I'm not sure she has ever taken a class on religious education. I know that she does not have a degree in that area.' While the parishioner acknowledged her own responsibility for the Catholic education of her children, she also wanted someone on the parish staff who was competent to assist her in that responsibility.

This concern was not an isolated example. We have heard similar concerns in a number of dioceses. The competency that is expected is not only in relationship to the initial education and training. Others have voiced their concern about members of the staff, clergy, laity, and religious who had been appointed at a time when they had all the prerequisite degrees. The concern was whether the staff had maintained their professional competence by participating in continuing education programs. As situations change and as the Church changes, new knowledge and skills are required. Leaders who do not continue to hone their competency soon become irrelevant. Most professional organizations, especially those that deal directly with the lives of people, demand updating and continuing education in order to retain a professional position. Are those working in the Church—dealing intimately with the lives and souls of individuals—required to prove their ongoing competency?

Whatever God does, the first outburst is always compassion.
—Meister Eckhart

It is the marriage of the two elements of competency and compassion that makes for effective leadership. When working in parishes, we frequently engage the parishioners in a process that we call the 'Ministry Needs Assessment.' We ask the participants to reflect on a time when they experienced ministry. As people share their experiences of ministry, it is evident how these experiences have been transformative. They share, often with great passion and emotion, how their lives have been touched by particular individuals. As we process the experiences of ministry and attempt to discern the essence of ministry, it inevitably emerges that the one constant is compassion. When someone is compassionate toward another, she or he truly touches the other. It is the competent, compassionate leaders who are most effective.

A Negative Example

We visited a school and met the principal, who had been working in education for more than twenty-five years. He had been a very good teacher and had achieved awards for his teaching. A few years ago, the previous principal retired. The present principal applied for the position and was hired. In listening to the teachers, it soon became clear that there was a high degree of frustration in the school. Both the teachers and parents were experiencing frustration. Although the principal was a fine teacher, he did not have the professional training, the gifts, or the competency to be an administrator, a principal, a leader of an educational community. He never acquired the training he needed to assume the role of principal. We later heard that the school board did not renew his contract. He was a very compassionate person and an excellent teacher, but was not a competent administrator.

A Positive Example

Many dioceses today are engaged in a process of evaluation and planning. In one diocese, concerns were voiced about the competency of the priests. The bishop met with the priests and shared the concern of the parishioners. Rather than react defensively, the priests discussed what they experienced and shared honestly and openly their being overwhelmed by the demands of their ever-changing ministry. After much discussion it was decided that the diocese would provide funding for each priest to receive supervision. Any priest could take advantage of the offer, but it was required of newly ordained priests, new pastors, and those in transition to new assignments. In reporting on their experience of supervision at a subsequent clergy conference, many priests reported how the personal supervision not only helped them to feel more confident in their ministry but also in their personal lives. The supervision had focused, not only on their ministry, but on their whole lives. To the many members of the diocese it was apparent that the priests had grown in confidence and in compassion.

Stop and Think

What have you done recently to strengthen your competency as a leader?

Can you recall a time when you experienced someone ministering to you? What was going on in your life? Who ministered to you? In what ways? Did you experience compassion?

Think of a recent encounter you had with someone in your role as leader. Would the other person or group involved describe you as compassionate? What do you have to do to grow more compassionate?

In Closing

<<<<<<<<<<<<<<<<<<<<<<<<<<<<<<<<<<<<<<<<<<<<<<<<<<<<<<<<<>

Personal Reflection

As you read through this book, there were probably a few of the principles that spoke to you in particularly poignant ways. These may be especially helpful to you in your continued growth as a leader in the Church. We encourage you to reflect on the following questions. If you choose to use the downloadable *Principled Ministry Workbook*, you will find these questions repeated there with room for you to write your responses.

1. What, if anything, surprised you in this book? How can you incorporate these newfound realizations into your ministry?

2. Which of the principles presented in this book would you consider the most important and why?

3. Which three principles from this book do you think you utilize most effectively in your ministry of leadership?

4. Identify three principles that you now believe are important for you to develop to improve your effectiveness as a Christian leader.

5. What additional principles would you add to our list of thirty and why?

Tracking Your Progress

We encourage you to use your responses to the third and fourth questions in the personal reflection as a jumping-off point for keeping a log of your progress in incorporating what you have learned from this book. We recommend spending time at the end of a day, reflecting on how you did as a leader that day. Keep a log to track the experience.

- Start with one or more of the principles about which you are already well disciplined (as identified in question 3 in the previous section) and then examine what other principles you used well that day. Describe the learning that occurred.
- Then, do the same with a principle you noted in your response to question 4 and examine how well you are improving in those areas.
- Repeat this simple exercise each day for a number of days or weeks that seems most helpful to you. Another alternative is to examine each week, rather than each day, but over a number of months.

◊ ◊ ◊

The following is an example of what such a log might look like.

List the principle, date, and your learning.

1. Set boundaries.

1/1/10

I met with one of the teachers today, a young, attractive woman who has been having trouble keeping control in the classroom. In the midst of the conference she began crying and telling me about the problems she was having in her marriage. I realized that I had a strong desire to put my arms around her and comfort her. I had to keep reminding myself that she is extremely vulnerable right now. I realized I had to maintain appropriate boundaries.

2. Trust your gut.

1/2/10

I had a potentially explosive staff meeting today. I spent time prior to the meeting recalling that my feelings would provide valuable information to me during the meeting. At one point during the meeting I could feel the tension escalating. I became aware that my tension was because of the fear of conflict erupting. Rather than simply emotionally withdrawing or reacting, I pulled back and used the feeling to help give me a clue as to how I could be helpful to the staff. I verbally acknowledged my tension and fear and said that I needed time to reflect on what was happening with me. I also indicated that perhaps it might be helpful for all of us to take a fifteen-minute break to reflect on what was happening within us.

When we returned we discussed the mutual fear, which was preventing us from listening to each other. That helped to defuse the tension and we had a very productive meeting. Because of this experience, I believe I will be more likely to trust my gut and respond, rather than simply react at the next meeting.

◊ ◊ ◊

To access the Principled Ministry Workbook, go to avemariapress.com and search for the book title, Principled Ministry. Once on the book product page, click the download button. You are welcome to print the 00-page workbook, free of additional charge.

Bibliography

◇◇

Albom, Mitch. *Tuesdays with Morrie.* Doubleday: New York, 1997

Armstrong, Terry R. 'Why the Bridge Hasn't Been Built and Other Profound Questions in Multicultural Organization Development' in *Change How We Manage Change.* Edited by Ronald R. Sims. Westport, CT: Quorum Books, 2002.

Bernardin, Joseph Cardinal. *The Gift of Peace.* Chicago: Loyola Press, 1997.

Carey, Michael. 'Transformative Christian Leadership,' *Human Development,* Vol. 12 No. 1, Spring 1991.

Clark, Carol. 'The Pastor as Vision Maker,' *Today's Parish,* September 1982.

Covey, Stephen. *The Seven Habits of Highly Effective People.* New York: Fireside, 1989.

Drucko, Paul and Marc Falenhain. 'Narcissism Sets Stage for Clergy Sexual Abuse,' *Human Development,* Vol.21, No. 3, Fall 2000.

Erikson, Erik. *Childhood and Society.* New York: W. W. Norton and Co. 1963.

Freidman, Edwin M. *Generation to Generation: Family Process in Church and Synagogue.* New York: The Guilford Press, 1985.

Hargrove, Robert. *Mastering the Art of Creative Collaboration.* New York: McGraw-Hill, 1998.

Kasper, Walter Cardinal. Fourth Annual Cardinal Bernardin Lecture, Silver Spring, MD, June 21, 2002. Printed in *Initiative Report: Catholic Common Ground Initiative,* Vol. 6, #3, September 2002.

Kennedy, Eugene, 'A Visit with Cardinal Joseph Bernardin,' *Notre Dame Magazine,* Autumn 1995.

Kennedy, Eugene *The Catholic Priest in the United States: Sociological Investigation.* Washington, DC: United States Conference of Catholic Bishops, 1972.

Libreria Editrice Vaticana. Catechism of the Catholic Church. Washington, DC: United States Conference of Catholic Bishops, 1994.

Mahony, Roger Cardinal. 'As I Have Done for You,' *Origins,* Vol. 29: No. 46. May 4, 2000.

Maslow, Abraham. *Toward a Psychology of Being.* New York: John Wiley and Sons, 1995.

Morrow, Lance. 'I Spoke as a Brother: A Pardon from the Pontiff, a Lesson in Forgiveness to a Troubled World,' *Time,* January 9, 1984.

Moustakas, Clark E. *Loneliness.* New York: Simon and Schuster: 1990.

Murnion, Philip, David De Lombo and Karen S. Smith, editors. *Parishes and Parish Ministers: A Study of Lay Ministry.* New York: National Pastoral Life Center, 1999.

Nygren, David and Miriam Ukeritis. 'Research Executive Summary: Future of Religious Orders in the United States,' *Origins,* Vol. 22: No. 15. September 24, 1992.

Pope John Paul II. 'Address to the Oblates of St. Joseph,' *L'Osservatore Romano*, March 8, 2000

Pope John Paul II. Redemptoris Missio (*On the Permanent Validity of the Church's Missionary Mandate*). Washington DC: United States Conference of Catholic Bishops, 1976.

Pope Paul VI. Evangelii Nuntiandi *(On Evangelization in the Modern World)*. Washington, DC: United States Conference of Catholic Bishops: Washington, DC, 1975.

Selye, Hans. *Stress without Distress.* Philadelphia, PA: Lippincott Williams & Wilkins, 1974.

Sofield, Loughlan, S.T., and Carroll Juliano, S.H.C.J. *Collaboration: Uniting Our Gifts in Ministry*. Notre Dame, IN: Ave Maria Press: 2000.

Sofield, Loughlan, S.T., and Donald Kuhn. *The Collaborative Leader: Listening to the Wisdom of God's People*. Notre Dame, IN: Ave Maria Press, 1995.

Sofield, Loughlan, S.T., Rosine Hammett, and Carroll Juliano, S.H.C.J. *Building Community: Christian, Caring, Vital.* Notre Dame, IN: Ave Maria Press, 1998.

————. *Design for Wholeness*. Notre Dame, IN: Ave Maria Press: 1990.

United States Conference of Catholic Bishops. *Called and Gifted for the Third Millennium*. Washington, DC: United States Conference of Catholic Bishops,1995.

Yalom, Irvin and Molyn Leszcz. The Theory and Practice of Group Psychotherapy. New York: Basic Books, 2005.

Zullo, James R., F.S.C., 'The Ministry of Referral,' *Human Development.* Vol 5: No 1, Spring 1984.